STERLING
New York

An Imprint of Sterling Publishing
387 Park Avenue South
New York, NY 10016

ISBN 978-1-4027-9148-2 (paperback)

Distributed in Canada by Sterling Publishing
c/o Canadian Manda Group, 165 Dufferin Street
Toronto, Ontario, Canada M6K 3H6
Distributed in the United Kingdom by GMC Distribution Services
Castle Place, 166 High Street, Lewes, East Sussex, England BN7 1XU
Distributed in Australia by Capricorn Link (Australia) Pty. Ltd.
P.O. Box 704, Windsor, NSW 2756, Australia

For information about custom editions, special sales, and premium and corporate purchases, please contact Sterling Special Sales at 800-805-5489 or specialsales@sterlingpublishing.com.

Manufactured in China

2 4 6 8 10 9 7 5 3 1

www.sterlingpublishing.com

DOLLAR BILL
ANOTHER WAY TO IMPRESS YOUR FRIENDS WITH MONEY
ORIGAMI

By DUY NGUYEN

STERLING
New York

CONTENTS

INTRODUCTION

Origami is a Japanese term that means "folding paper." This centuries-old art form of folding paper into sculptures traditionally uses square pieces of paper with colors or prints on one side of the paper. However, there's no hard-and-fast rule that you can *only* fold with square paper. In fact, you can create amazing paper sculptures using any size or shape piece of paper—including paper currency. I've found dollar bills to be an incredibly creative medium (dollar bill origami figures make great gifts—and tips!), and I'm delighted to share the eighteen designs in this book with you.

When I first began to fold origami, I found it difficult to follow most instructions. I would have to look at even the simplest folds given at the beginning of the book again and again. But I also looked ahead at the diagram showing the next step of whatever project I was folding to see how it should look. As it turned out, that was the right thing to do. Looking ahead at the next step—the result of a fold—is a very good way for beginners to learn origami.

You will easily pick up this and other techniques as you follow the step-by-step instructions given here for making all your dollar bill origami figures. And once you have these under your belt, there's nothing to stop you from creating your own designs. So sit down, grab some money, and enjoy the priceless art that is dollar bill origami!

—Duy Nguyen

THE BILLS: All the projects in *Dollar Bill Origami* are specially designed to be folded with paper currency. Any denomination will work, and you can find sample dollar-sized paper at the back of this book to get you started. (Most paper currency around the world is rectangular, so, with a little adjusting, you can make these figures with money from most countries.) As you may have figured out already, the crisper the bill, the better. Old, worn bills will not hold their folds all that well, so I suggest that you head to the nearest bank and trade in your old bills for brand-new ones. If you have some bills that are in okay shape, you can rinse, dry, and then iron them on medium heat. If you want to use different paper for these projects, U.S. currency is 2.61" x 6.14."

NOTE: U.S. paper currency is actually government property, and although it is legal to fold paper money, you cannot cut, tear, or glue it. (A little piece of tape every now and then is probably fine.)

SETTING FOLDS: Even without using glue, there are ways to set your folds. You can use an iron on medium heat to set folds or to set an entire figure. You can also use a little piece of double-stick tape to keep folds together as well as to keep multi-bill projects from falling apart. Finally, small paper clips can be placed on folds to set them.

TECHNIQUE: Fold with care. Position the dollar bill precisely and line the edges up before creasing. Once you are sure of the fold, use a fingernail to make a clean, flat crease. For more complex folds, create "construction lines." Fold and unfold, using simple mountain and valley folds, to pre-crease. This creates construction lines, and the finished fold is more likely to match the one shown in the book. Don't get discouraged with your first efforts. In time, what your mind can create, your fingers can fashion.

CREATIVITY: If you fold a favorite project several times, do you really want them all to look exactly alike? Once you are more comfortable with your folding ability, try adjusting certain folds to shape the form more to your liking, bringing each project to life in your hands.

BASIC FOLDS & SYMBOLS

LEGEND

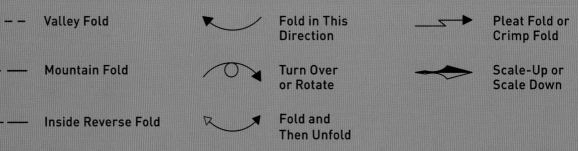

- – – – –   Valley Fold

— – – —   Mountain Fold

— – · —   Inside Reverse Fold

Fold in This Direction

Turn Over or Rotate

Fold and Then Unfold

Pleat Fold or Crimp Fold

Scale-Up or Scale Down

VALLEY FOLD

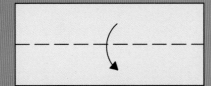

1. Fold forward.

2. Completed Valley Fold.

MOUNTAIN FOLD

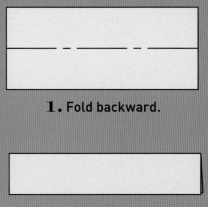

1. Fold backward.

2. Completed Mountain Fold.

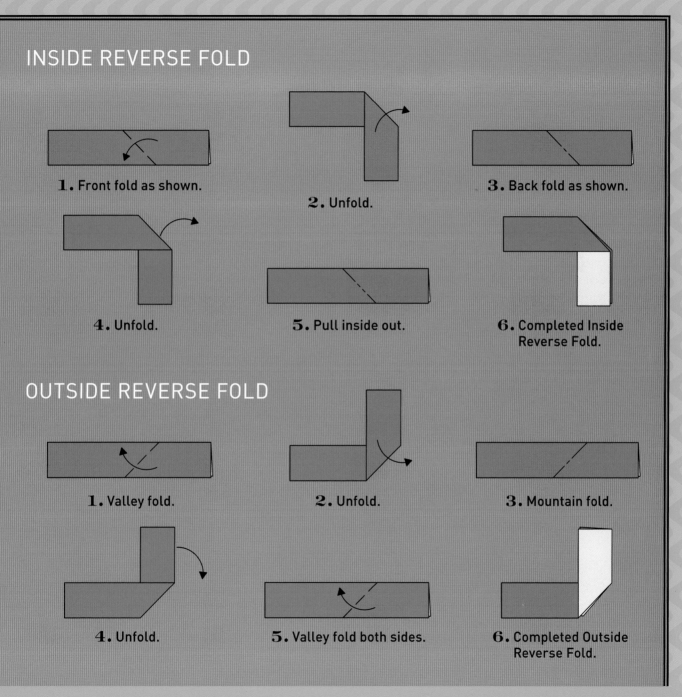

INSIDE REVERSE FOLD

1. Front fold as shown.

2. Unfold.

3. Back fold as shown.

4. Unfold.

5. Pull inside out.

6. Completed Inside Reverse Fold.

OUTSIDE REVERSE FOLD

1. Valley fold.

2. Unfold.

3. Mountain fold.

4. Unfold.

5. Valley fold both sides.

6. Completed Outside Reverse Fold.

SQUASH FOLD 1

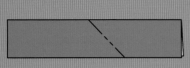

1. Inside reverse fold.

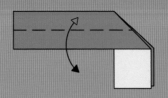

2. Valley fold and unfold.

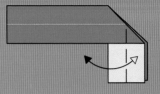

3. Valley fold and unfold.

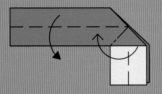

4. Valley folds and inside reverse fold at the same time.

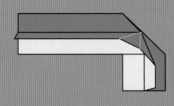

5. Before complete.

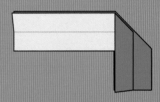

6. Completed Squash Fold 1.

SQUASH FOLD 2

1. Inside reverse fold.

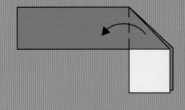

2. Valley fold.

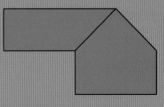

3. Completed Squash Fold 2.

PLEAT FOLD

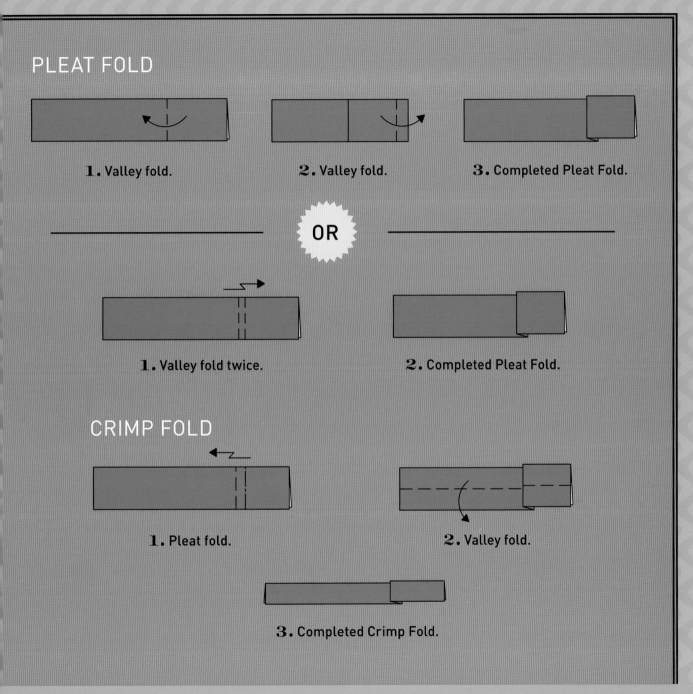

1. Valley fold.

2. Valley fold.

3. Completed Pleat Fold.

OR

1. Valley fold twice.

2. Completed Pleat Fold.

CRIMP FOLD

1. Pleat fold.

2. Valley fold.

3. Completed Crimp Fold.

BASE FOLD

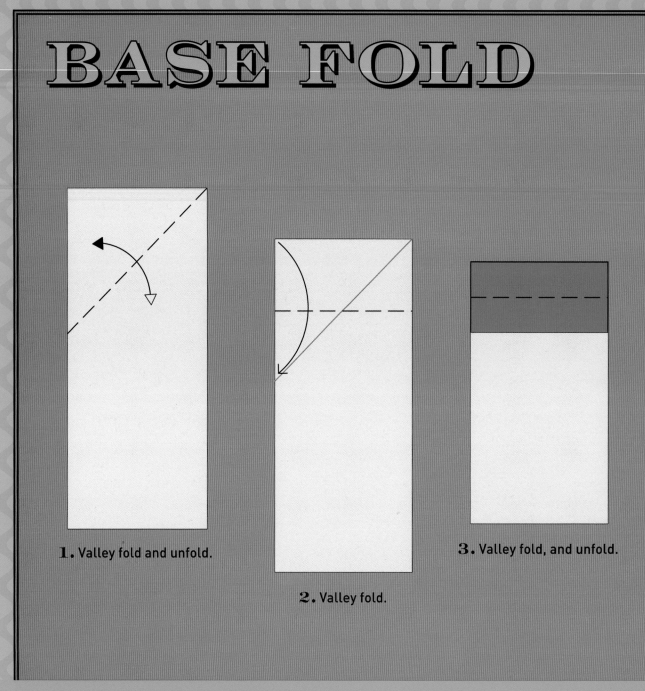

1. Valley fold and unfold.

2. Valley fold.

3. Valley fold, and unfold.

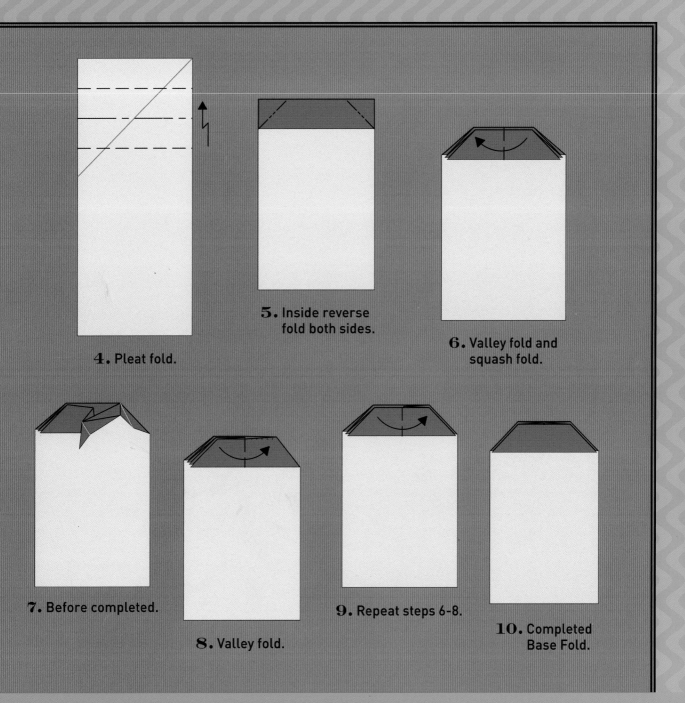

4. Pleat fold.

5. Inside reverse fold both sides.

6. Valley fold and squash fold.

7. Before completed.

8. Valley fold.

9. Repeat steps 6-8.

10. Completed Base Fold.

PUSHPIN

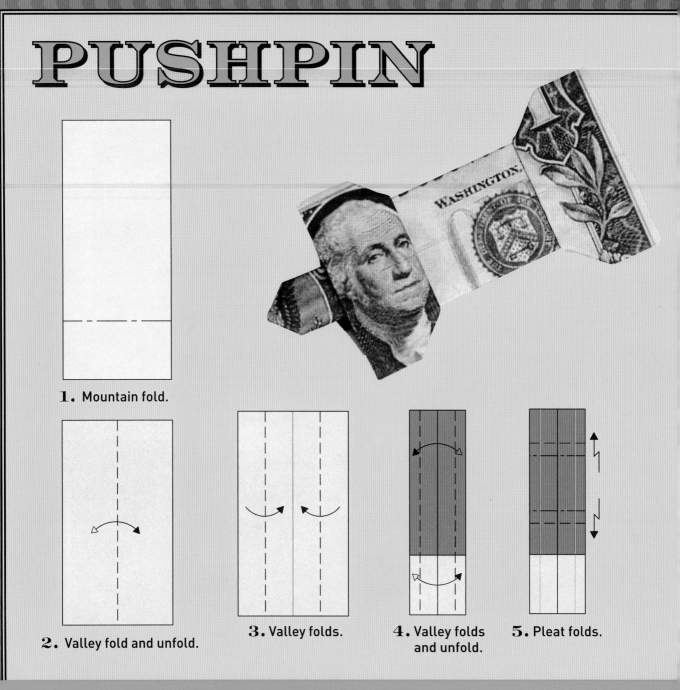

1. Mountain fold.

2. Valley fold and unfold.

3. Valley folds.

4. Valley folds and unfold.

5. Pleat folds.

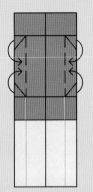

6. Squash folds.

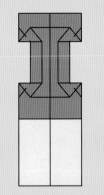

7. Valley folds.

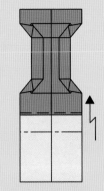

8. Pleat fold.

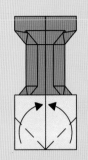

9. Valley folds.

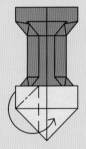

10. Squash fold.

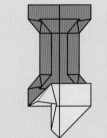

11. Before completed.

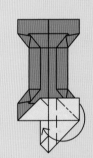

12. Hide behind layer.

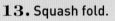

13. Squash fold.

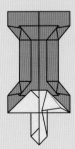

14. Before completed.

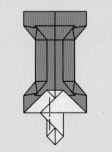

15. Mountain fold.

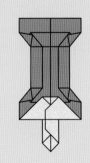

16. Turn over.

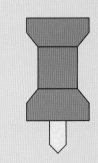

17. Completed Pushpin.

PIPE

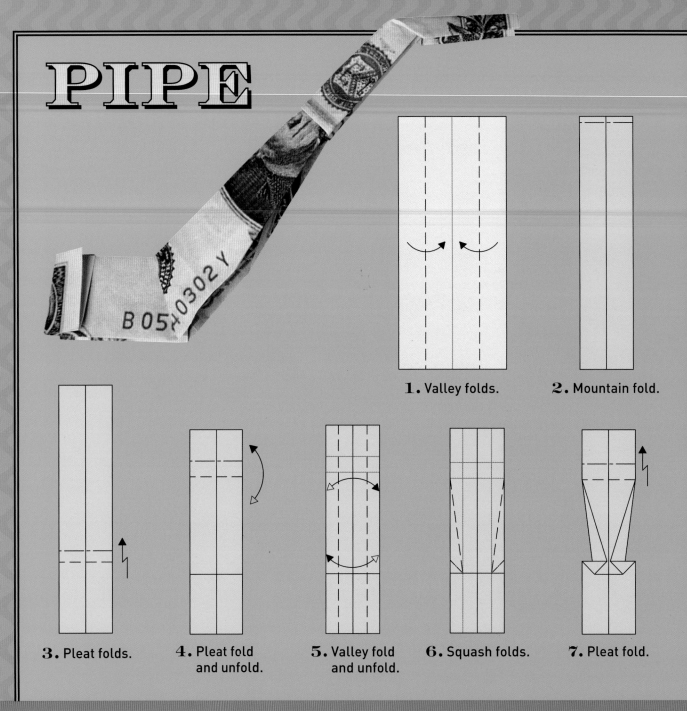

1. Valley folds.

2. Mountain fold.

3. Pleat folds.

4. Pleat fold and unfold.

5. Valley fold and unfold.

6. Squash folds.

7. Pleat fold.

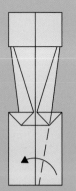

8. Valley fold.

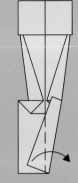

9. Repeat.

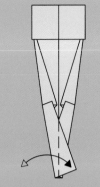

10. Valley fold.

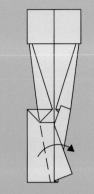

11. Valley fold and unfold.

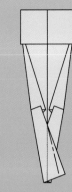

12. Mountain fold.

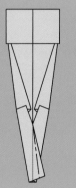

13. Mountain folds.

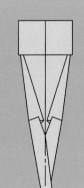

14. Mountain fold.

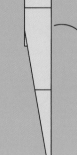

15. Mountain fold.

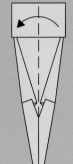

16. Pull and fold.

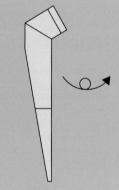

17. Rotate.

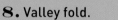

18. Inside reverse fold.

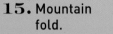
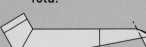

19. Valley fold the front.

20. Mountain fold the back.

21. Completed Pipe.

GUN & HOLSTER

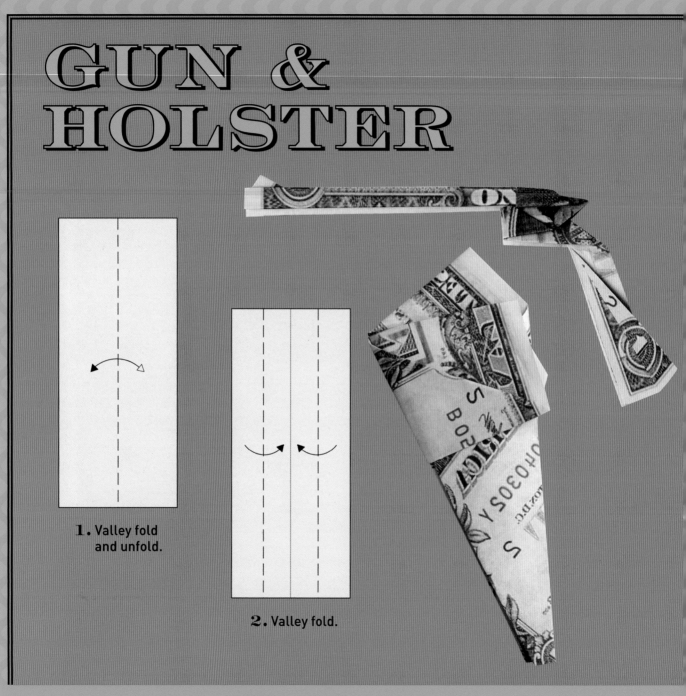

1. Valley fold and unfold.

2. Valley fold.

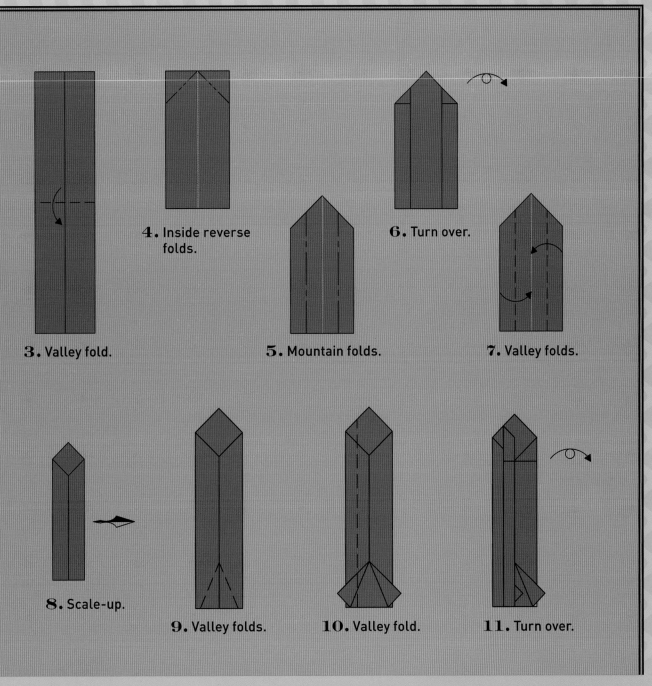

3. Valley fold.

4. Inside reverse folds.

5. Mountain folds.

6. Turn over.

7. Valley folds.

8. Scale-up.

9. Valley folds.

10. Valley fold.

11. Turn over.

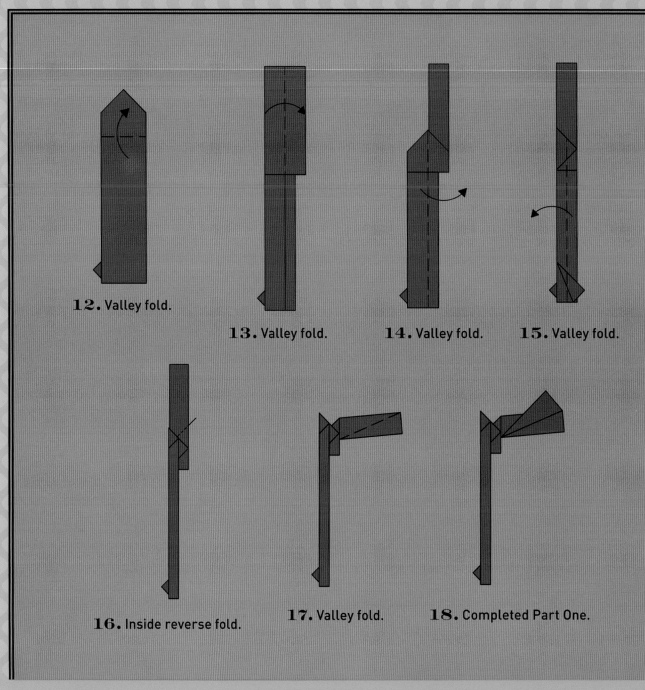

12. Valley fold.

13. Valley fold.

14. Valley fold.

15. Valley fold.

16. Inside reverse fold.

17. Valley fold.

18. Completed Part One.

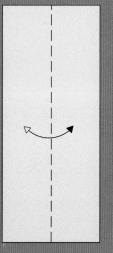

1. Valley fold and unfold.

2. Valley folds.

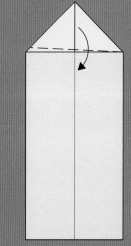

3. Valley fold.

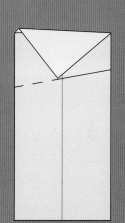

4. Mountain fold.

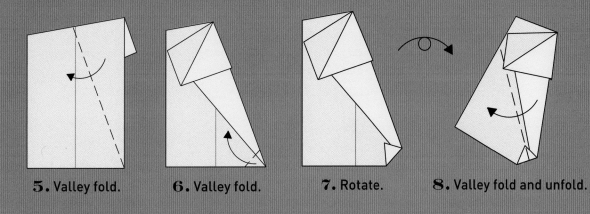

5. Valley fold.

6. Valley fold.

7. Rotate.

8. Valley fold and unfold.

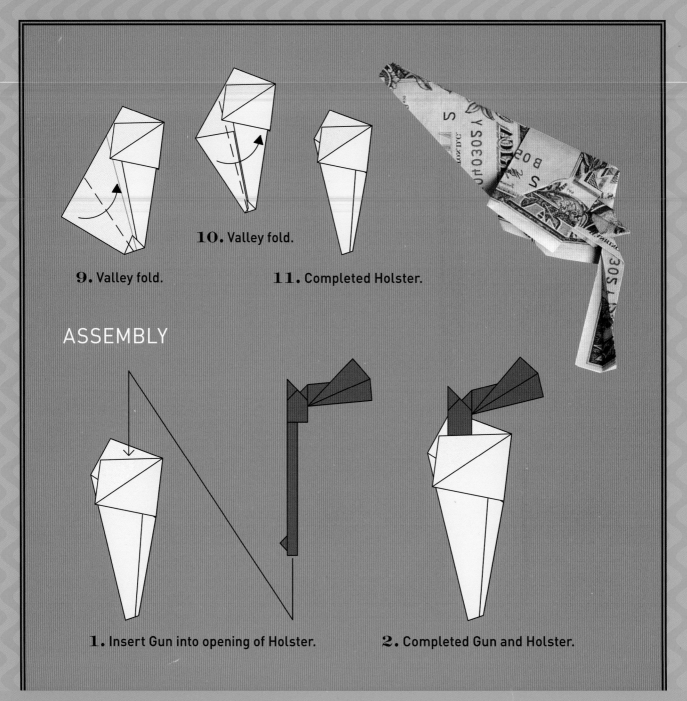

9. Valley fold.

10. Valley fold.

11. Completed Holster.

ASSEMBLY

1. Insert Gun into opening of Holster.

2. Completed Gun and Holster.

PEN

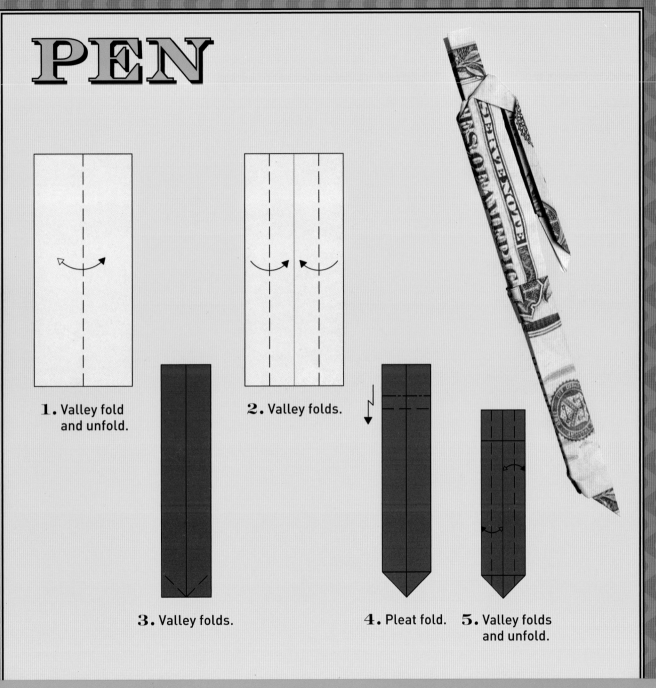

1. Valley fold and unfold.

2. Valley folds.

3. Valley folds.

4. Pleat fold.

5. Valley folds and unfold.

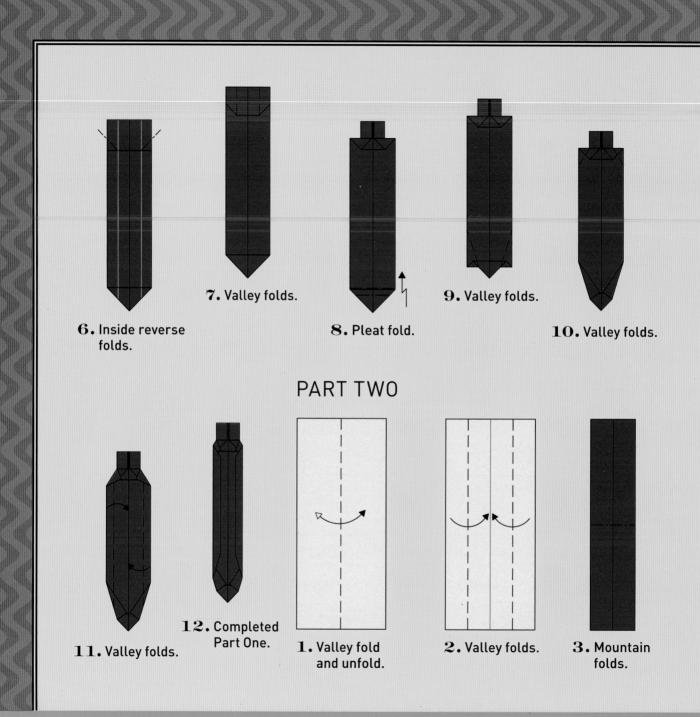

6. Inside reverse folds.

7. Valley folds.

8. Pleat fold.

9. Valley folds.

10. Valley folds.

PART TWO

11. Valley folds.

12. Completed Part One.

1. Valley fold and unfold.

2. Valley folds.

3. Mountain folds.

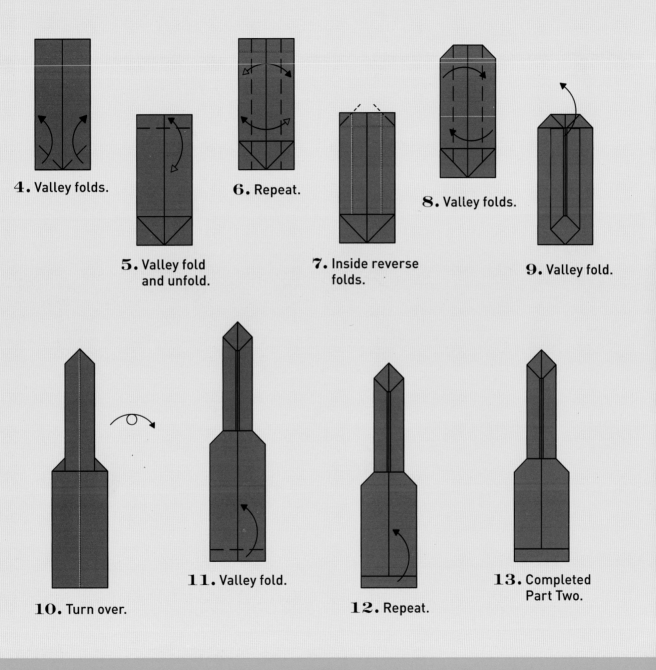

4. Valley folds.

5. Valley fold and unfold.

6. Repeat.

7. Inside reverse folds.

8. Valley folds.

9. Valley fold.

10. Turn over.

11. Valley fold.

12. Repeat.

13. Completed Part Two.

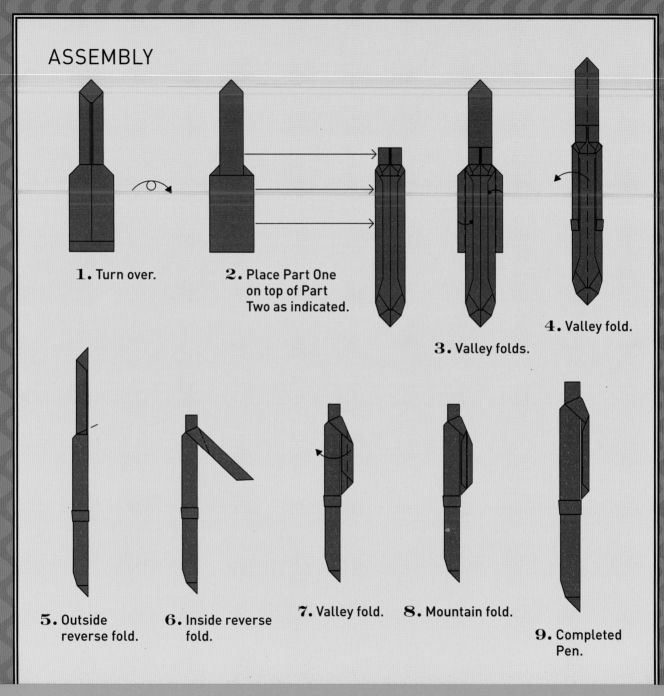

ASSEMBLY

1. Turn over.

2. Place Part One on top of Part Two as indicated.

3. Valley folds.

4. Valley fold.

5. Outside reverse fold.

6. Inside reverse fold.

7. Valley fold.

8. Mountain fold.

9. Completed Pen.

POLAR BEAR

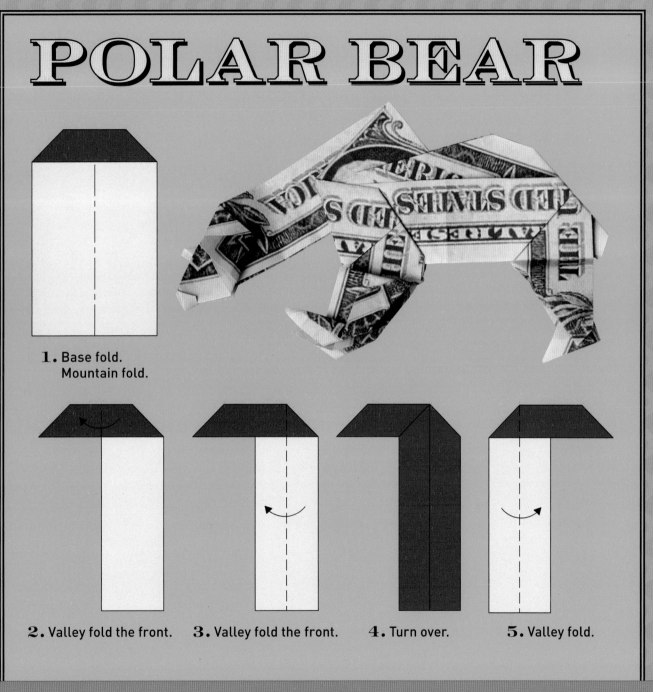

1. Base fold.
Mountain fold.

2. Valley fold the front.

3. Valley fold the front.

4. Turn over.

5. Valley fold.

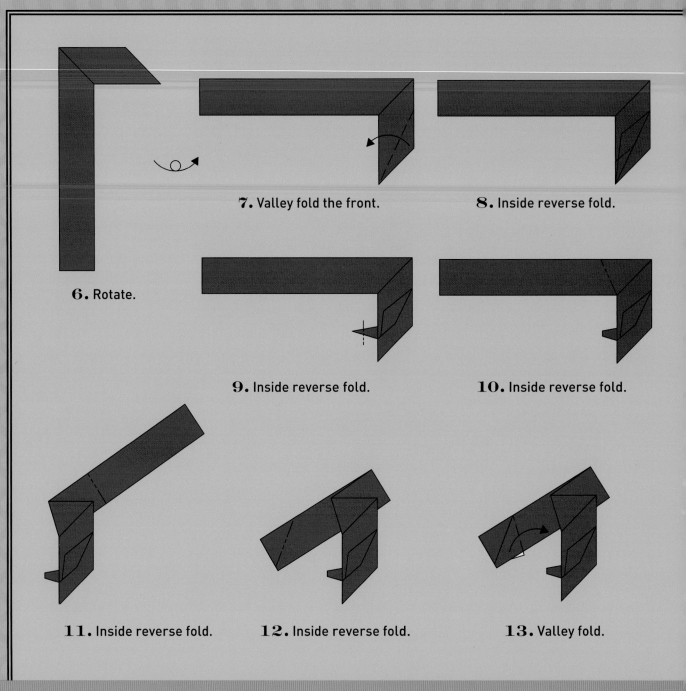

6. Rotate.

7. Valley fold the front.

8. Inside reverse fold.

9. Inside reverse fold.

10. Inside reverse fold.

11. Inside reverse fold.

12. Inside reverse fold.

13. Valley fold.

14. Valley fold.

15. Turn over.

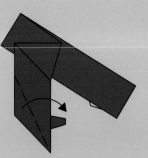

16. Valley fold.

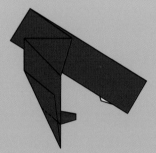

17. Inside reverse fold.

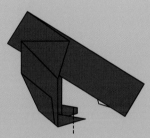

18. Inside reverse fold.

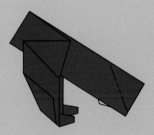

19. Inside reverse fold.

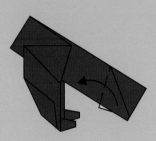

20. Valley fold.

21. Valley fold.

22. Completed Part One.

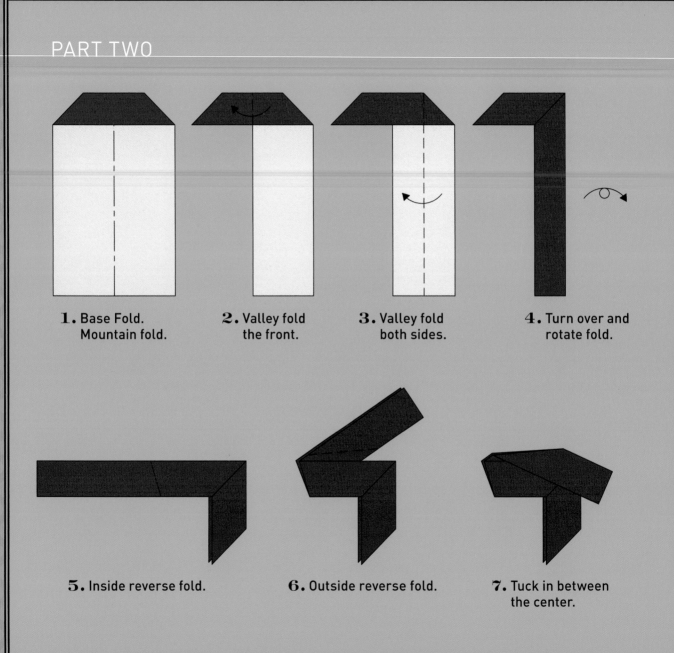

1. Base Fold.
   Mountain fold.

2. Valley fold
   the front.

3. Valley fold
   both sides.

4. Turn over and
   rotate fold.

5. Inside reverse fold.

6. Outside reverse fold.

7. Tuck in between
   the center.

8. Inside reverse fold.

9. Pleat fold both the front and the back.

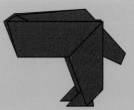

10. Completed Part Two.

ASSEMBLY

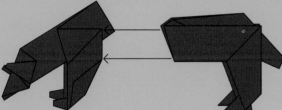

1. Insert as indicated by the arrows.

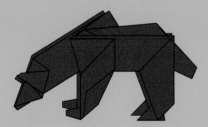

2. Mountain fold both at the tail and thigh to help the two parts hold together.

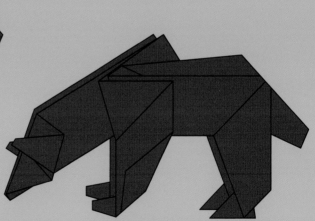

3. Completed Polar Bear.

ELEPHANT

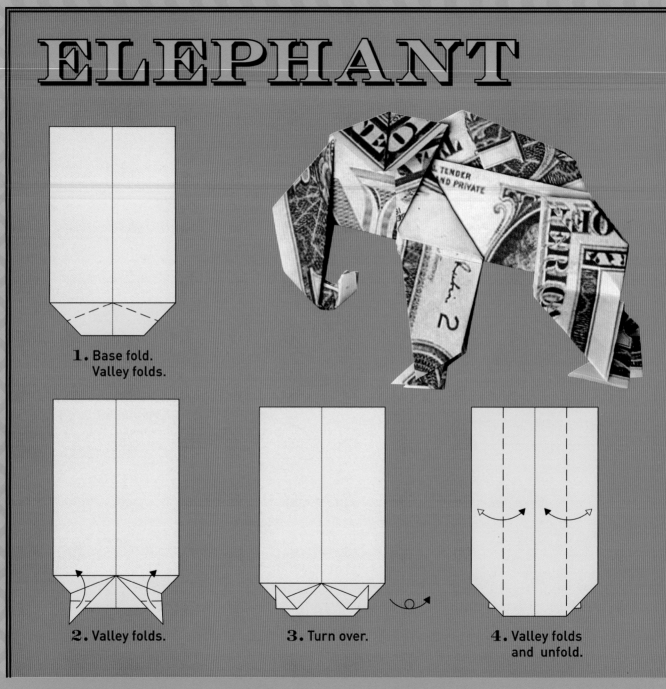

1. Base fold.
Valley folds.

2. Valley folds.

3. Turn over.

4. Valley folds
and unfold.

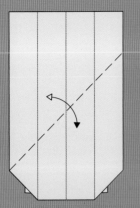

5. Valley fold and unfold.

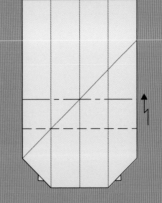

6. Pleat fold.

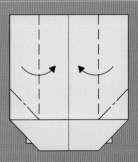

7. Squash folds.

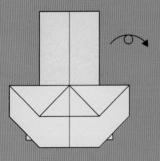

8. Turn over.

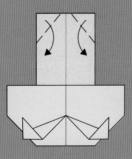

9. Valley folds.

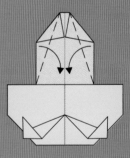

10. Valley folds.

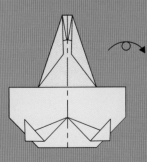

11. Mountain folds and rotate.

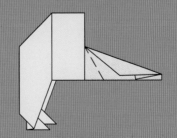

12. Outside reverse fold.

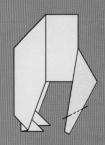

13. Inside reverse fold.

ELEPHANT

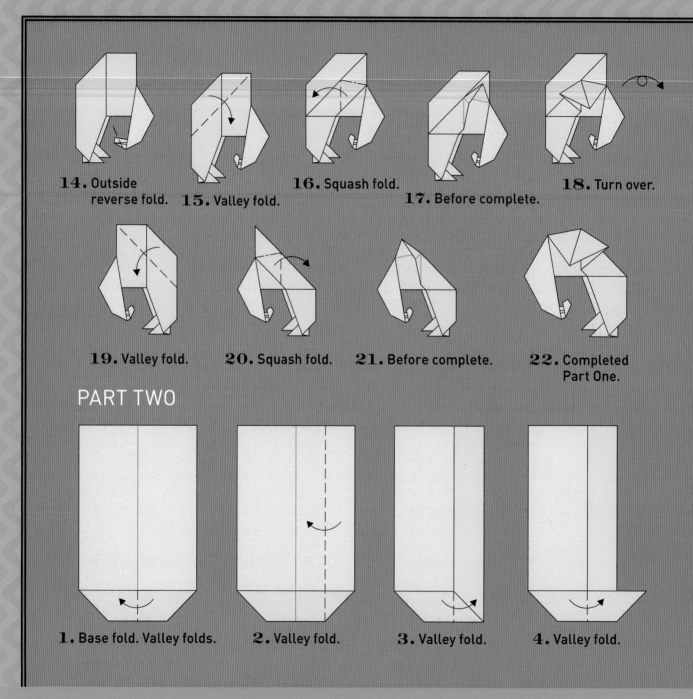

14. Outside reverse fold. **15.** Valley fold. **16.** Squash fold. **17.** Before complete. **18.** Turn over.

19. Valley fold. **20.** Squash fold. **21.** Before complete. **22.** Completed Part One.

PART TWO

1. Base fold. Valley folds. **2.** Valley fold. **3.** Valley fold. **4.** Valley fold.

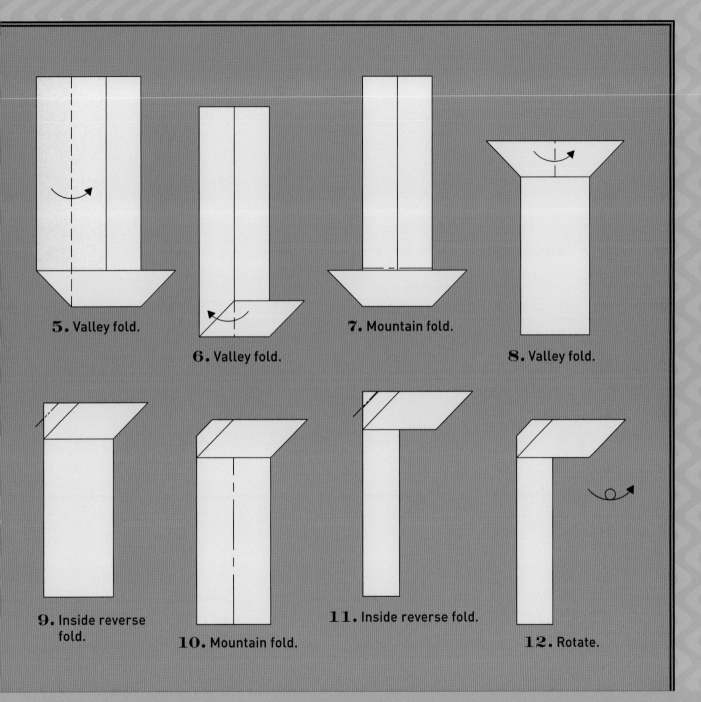

5. Valley fold.

6. Valley fold.

7. Mountain fold.

8. Valley fold.

9. Inside reverse fold.

10. Mountain fold.

11. Inside reverse fold.

12. Rotate.

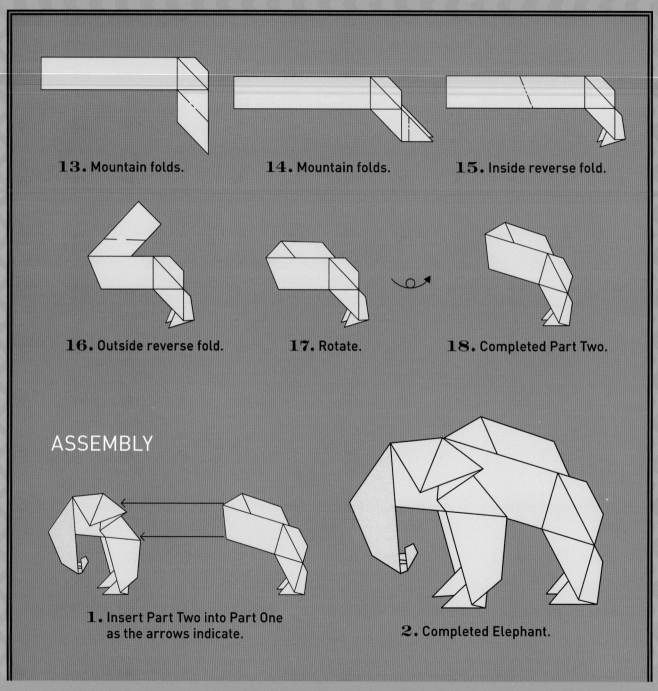

13. Mountain folds.

14. Mountain folds.

15. Inside reverse fold.

16. Outside reverse fold.

17. Rotate.

18. Completed Part Two.

ASSEMBLY

1. Insert Part Two into Part One as the arrows indicate.

2. Completed Elephant.

MERMAID

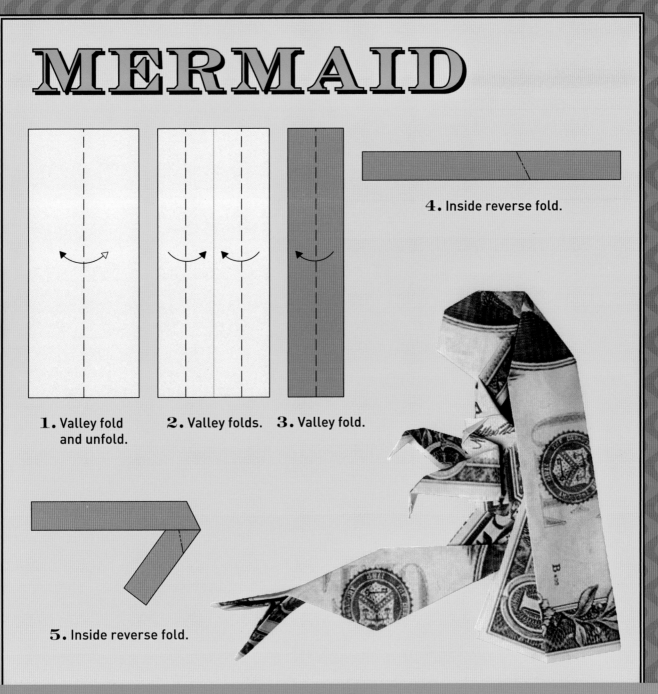

1. Valley fold and unfold.

2. Valley folds.

3. Valley fold.

4. Inside reverse fold.

5. Inside reverse fold.

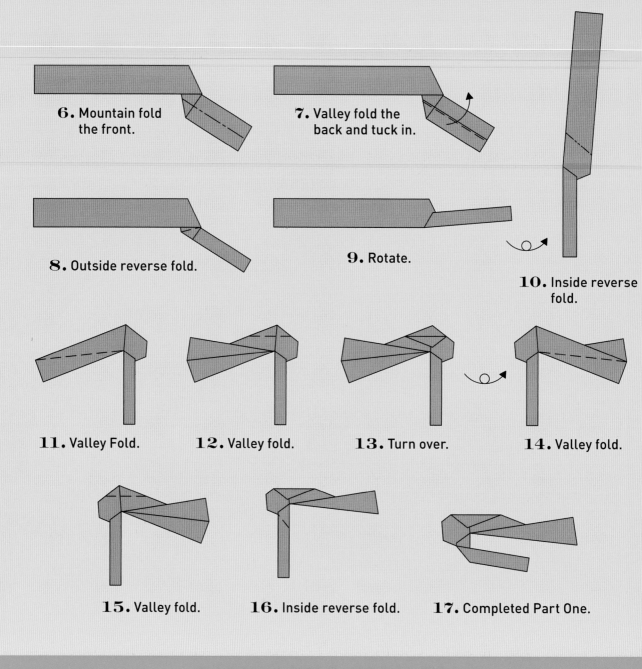

6. Mountain fold the front.

7. Valley fold the back and tuck in.

8. Outside reverse fold.

9. Rotate.

10. Inside reverse fold.

11. Valley Fold.

12. Valley fold.

13. Turn over.

14. Valley fold.

15. Valley fold.

16. Inside reverse fold.

17. Completed Part One.

PART TWO

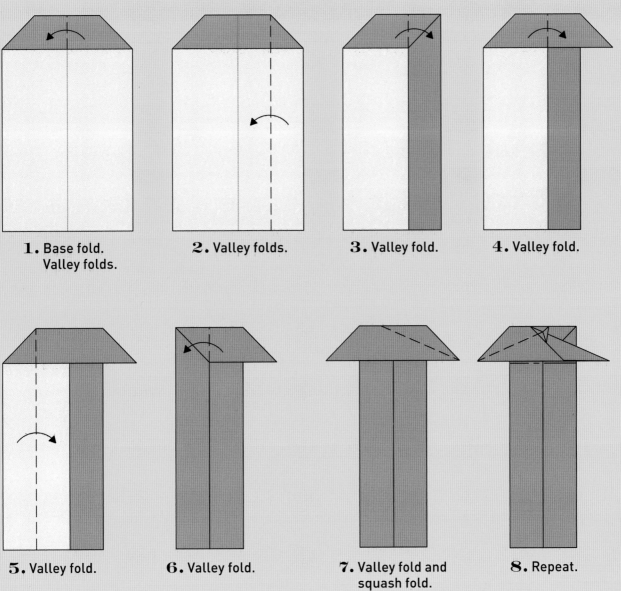

1. Base fold.
   Valley folds.

2. Valley folds.

3. Valley fold.

4. Valley fold.

5. Valley fold.

6. Valley fold.

7. Valley fold and
   squash fold.

8. Repeat.

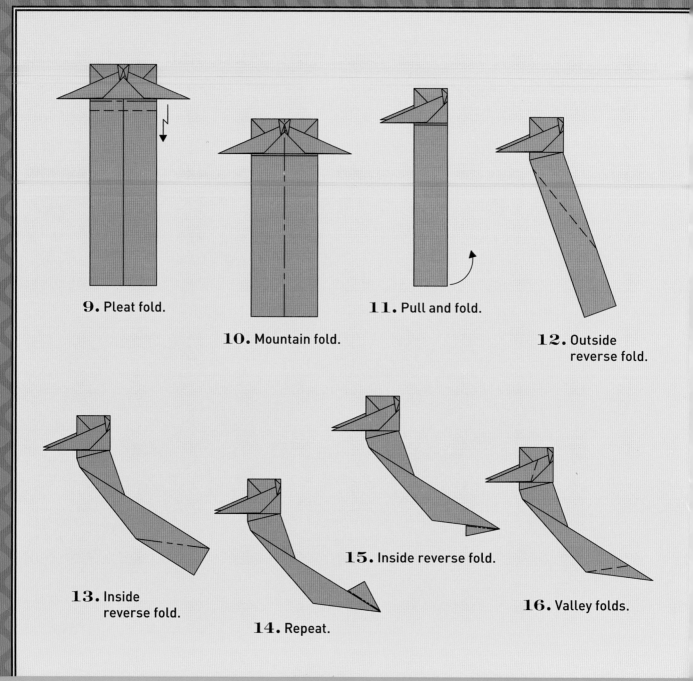

9. Pleat fold.

10. Mountain fold.

11. Pull and fold.

12. Outside reverse fold.

13. Inside reverse fold.

14. Repeat.

15. Inside reverse fold.

16. Valley folds.

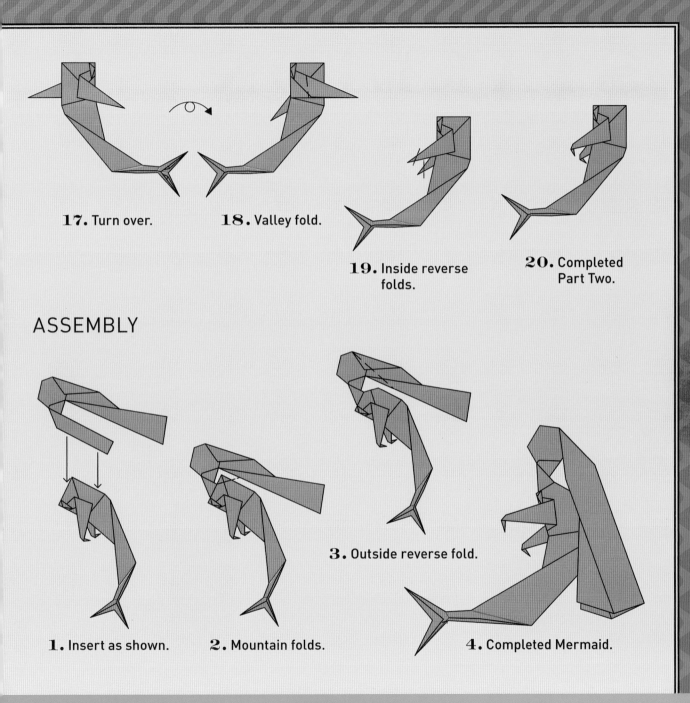

17. Turn over.

18. Valley fold.

19. Inside reverse folds.

20. Completed Part Two.

ASSEMBLY

1. Insert as shown.

2. Mountain folds.

3. Outside reverse fold.

4. Completed Mermaid.

STALLION

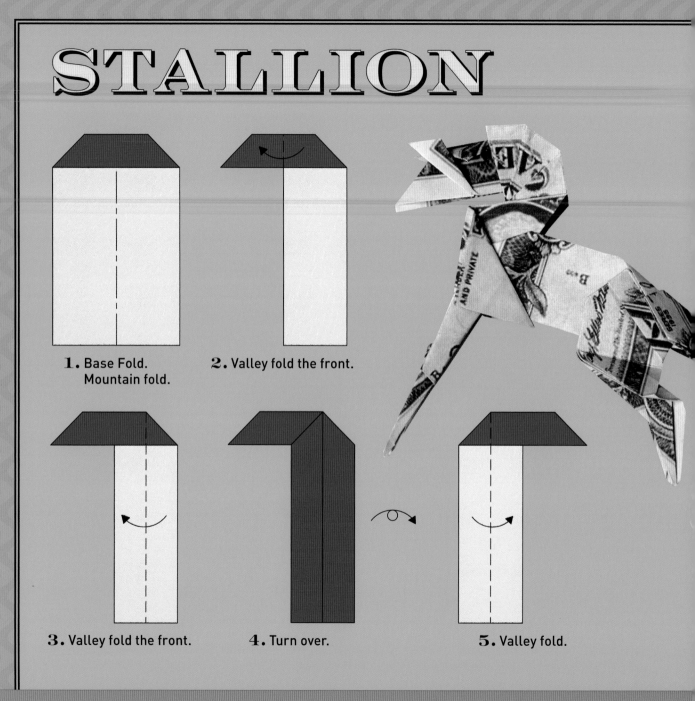

1. Base Fold.
Mountain fold.

2. Valley fold the front.

3. Valley fold the front.

4. Turn over.

5. Valley fold.

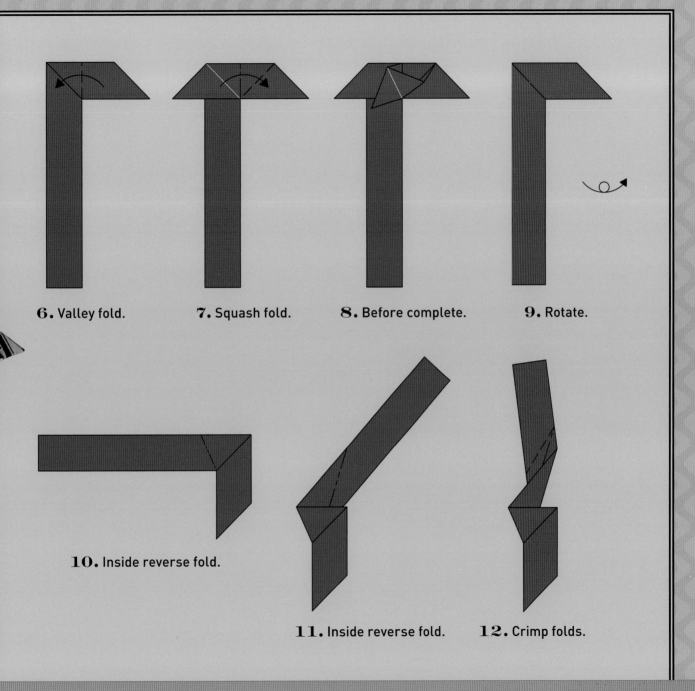

6. Valley fold.

7. Squash fold.

8. Before complete.

9. Rotate.

10. Inside reverse fold.

11. Inside reverse fold.

12. Crimp folds.

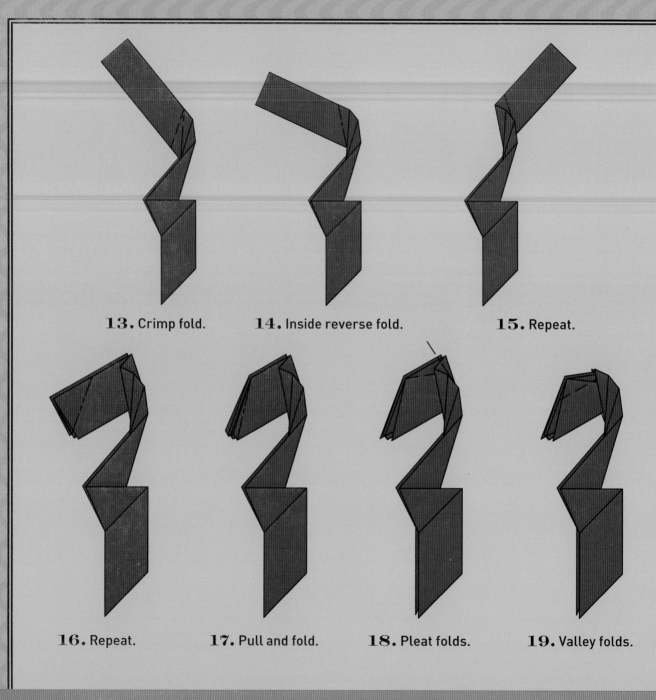

13. Crimp fold.

14. Inside reverse fold.

15. Repeat.

16. Repeat.

17. Pull and fold.

18. Pleat folds.

19. Valley folds.

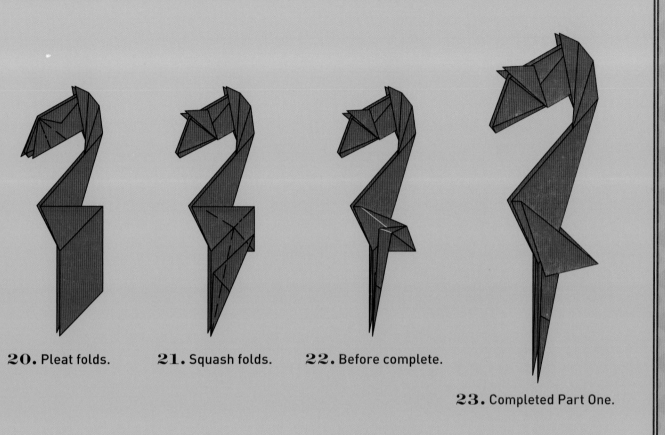

20. Pleat folds.

21. Squash folds.

22. Before complete.

23. Completed Part One.

PART TWO

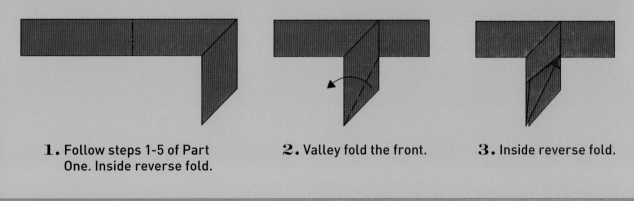

1. Follow steps 1-5 of Part One. Inside reverse fold.

2. Valley fold the front.

3. Inside reverse fold.

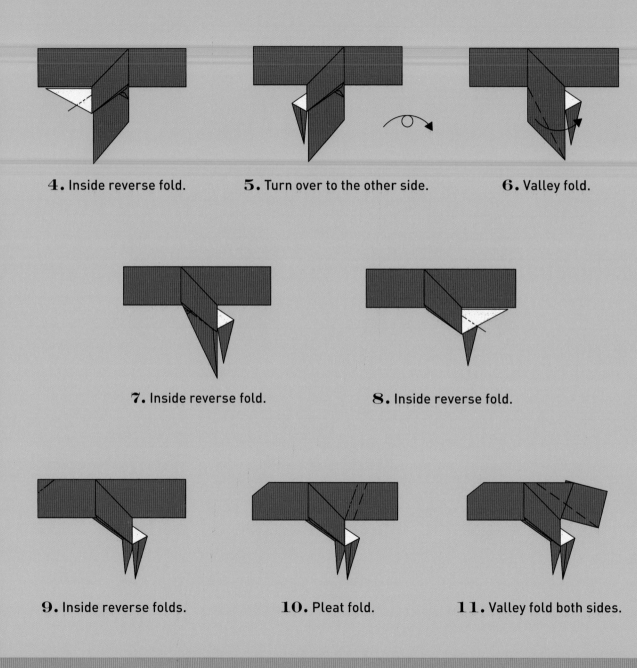

4. Inside reverse fold.

5. Turn over to the other side.

6. Valley fold.

7. Inside reverse fold.

8. Inside reverse fold.

9. Inside reverse folds.

10. Pleat fold.

11. Valley fold both sides.

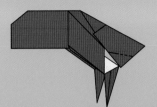

12. Inside reverse fold the front.

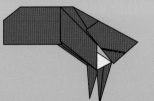

13. Inside reverse fold the back.

14. Completed Part Two.

ASSEMBLY

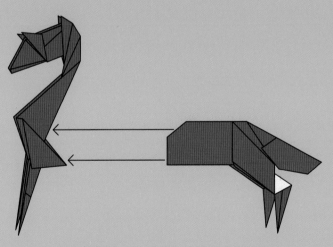

1. Insert Part Two into Part One as shown.

2. Completed Stallion.

GERMAN SHEPHERD

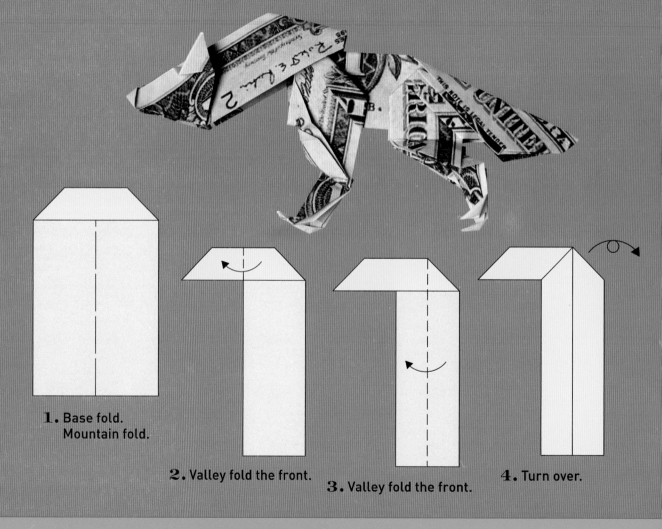

1. Base fold.
   Mountain fold.

2. Valley fold the front.

3. Valley fold the front.

4. Turn over.

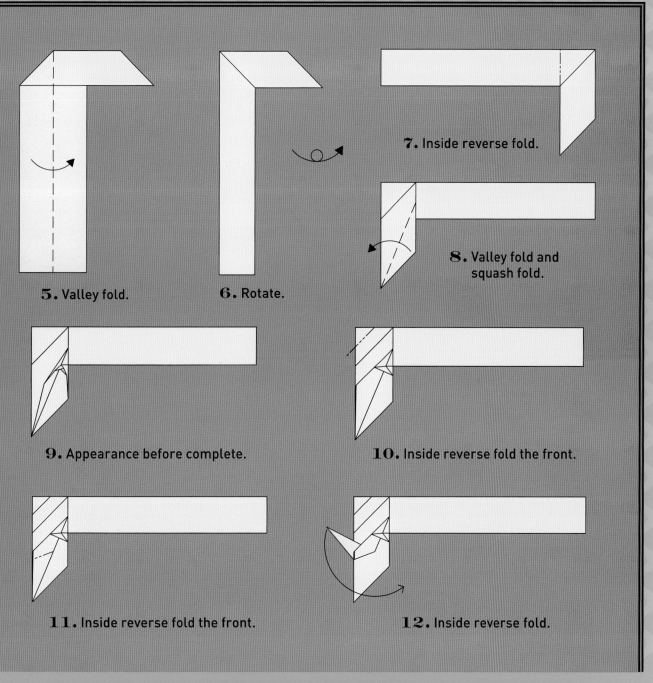

5. Valley fold.

6. Rotate.

7. Inside reverse fold.

8. Valley fold and squash fold.

9. Appearance before complete.

10. Inside reverse fold the front.

11. Inside reverse fold the front.

12. Inside reverse fold.

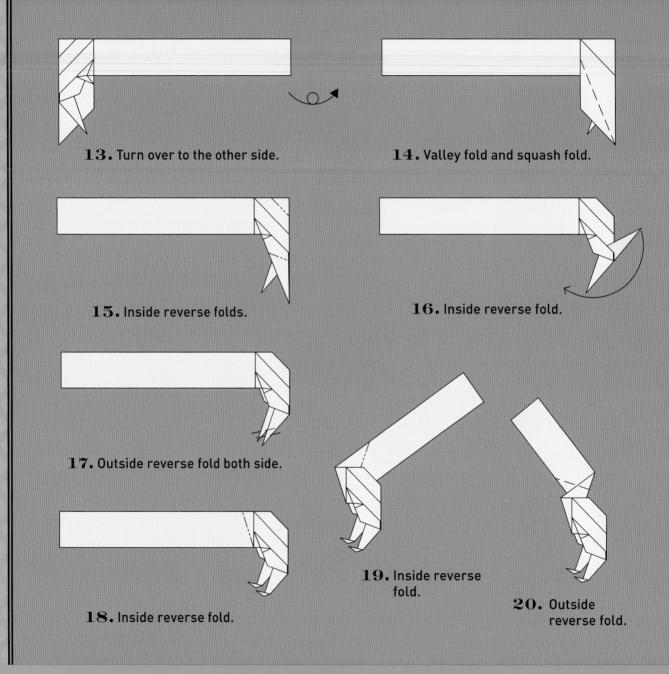

13. Turn over to the other side.

14. Valley fold and squash fold.

15. Inside reverse folds.

16. Inside reverse fold.

17. Outside reverse fold both side.

19. Inside reverse fold.

18. Inside reverse fold.

20. Outside reverse fold.

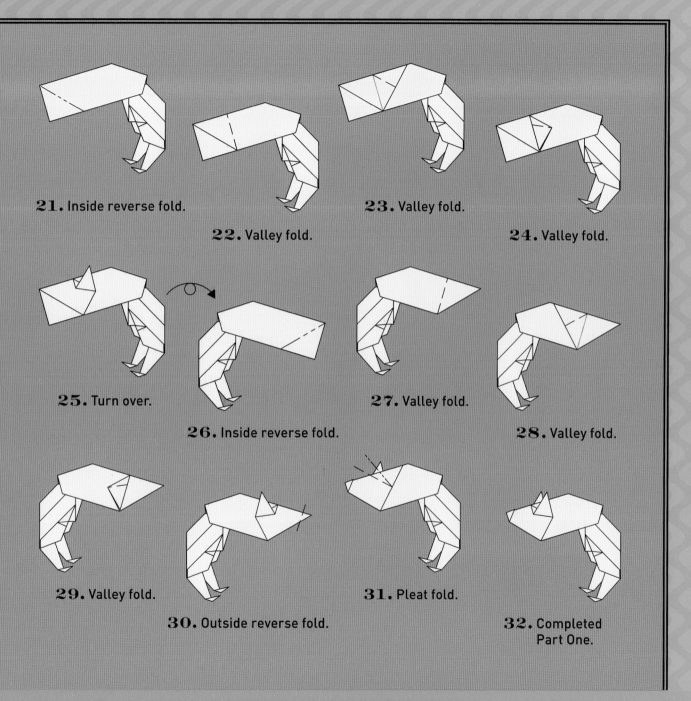

21. Inside reverse fold.

22. Valley fold.

23. Valley fold.

24. Valley fold.

25. Turn over.

26. Inside reverse fold.

27. Valley fold.

28. Valley fold.

29. Valley fold.

30. Outside reverse fold.

31. Pleat fold.

32. Completed Part One.

GERMAN SHEPHERD

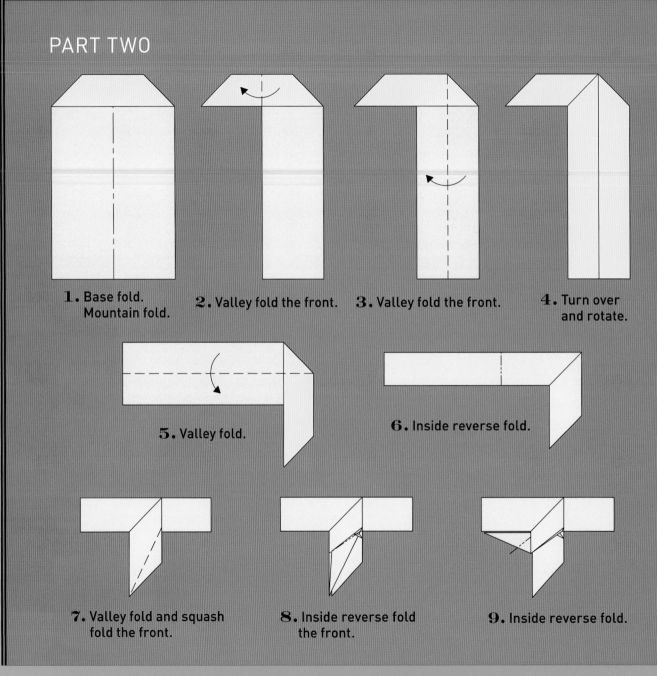

1. Base fold. Mountain fold.

2. Valley fold the front.

3. Valley fold the front.

4. Turn over and rotate.

5. Valley fold.

6. Inside reverse fold.

7. Valley fold and squash fold the front.

8. Inside reverse fold the front.

9. Inside reverse fold.

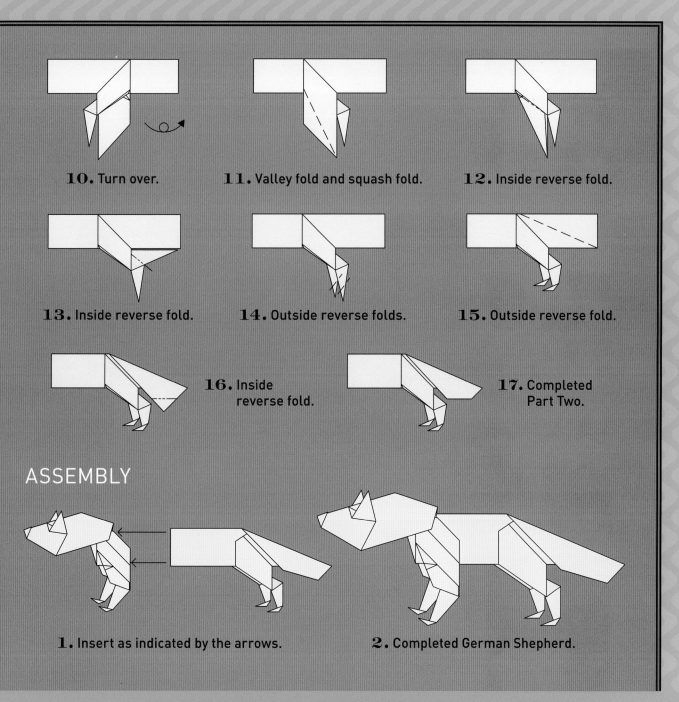

10. Turn over.

11. Valley fold and squash fold.

12. Inside reverse fold.

13. Inside reverse fold.

14. Outside reverse folds.

15. Outside reverse fold.

16. Inside reverse fold.

17. Completed Part Two.

ASSEMBLY

1. Insert as indicated by the arrows.

2. Completed German Shepherd.

SQUIRREL

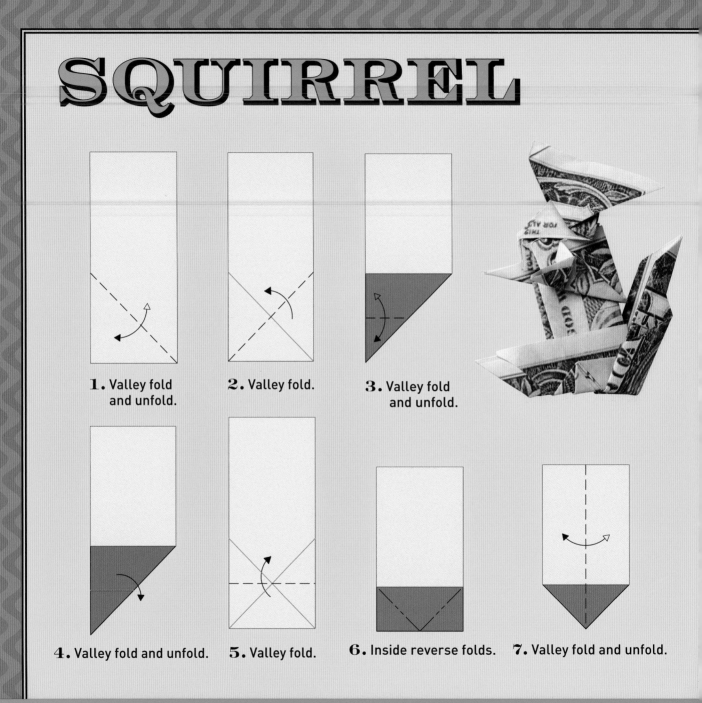

1. Valley fold and unfold.

2. Valley fold.

3. Valley fold and unfold.

4. Valley fold and unfold.

5. Valley fold.

6. Inside reverse folds.

7. Valley fold and unfold.

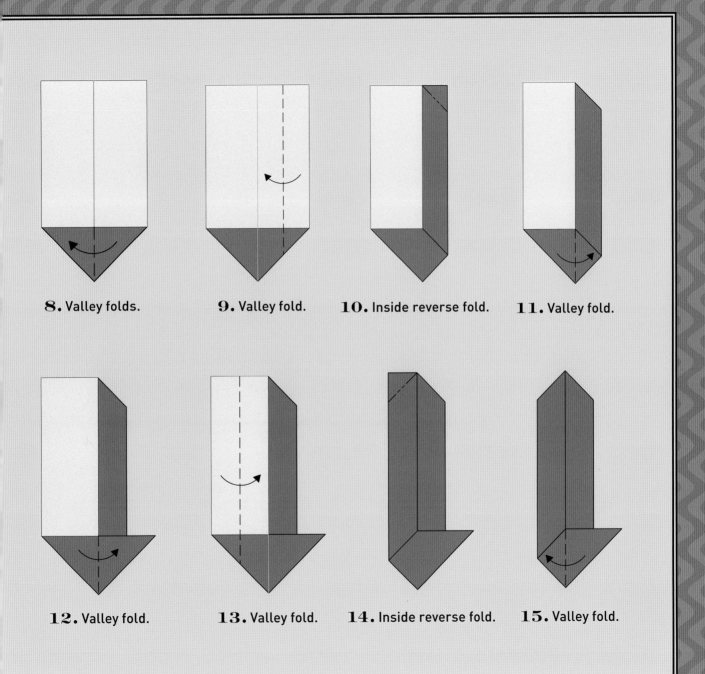

8. Valley folds.

9. Valley fold.

10. Inside reverse fold.

11. Valley fold.

12. Valley fold.

13. Valley fold.

14. Inside reverse fold.

15. Valley fold.

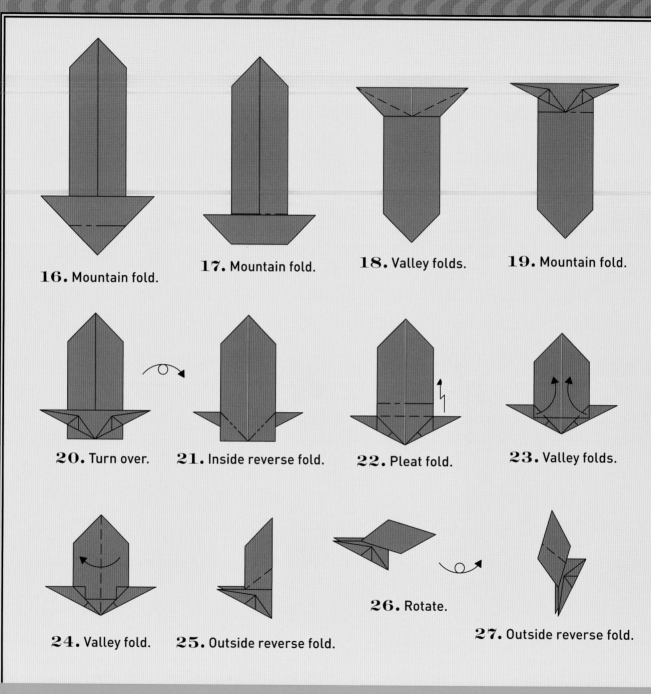

16. Mountain fold.

17. Mountain fold.

18. Valley folds.

19. Mountain fold.

20. Turn over.

21. Inside reverse fold.

22. Pleat fold.

23. Valley folds.

24. Valley fold.

25. Outside reverse fold.

26. Rotate.

27. Outside reverse fold.

DOLLAR BILL ORIGAMI

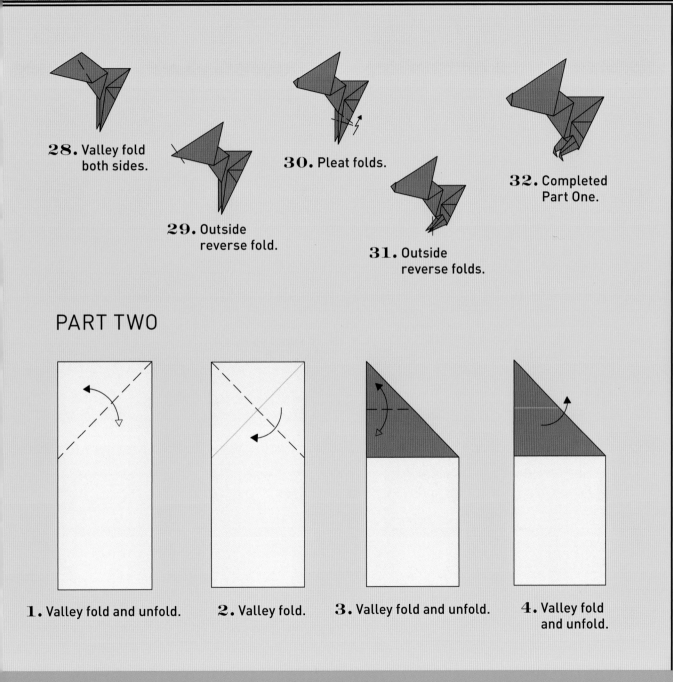

28. Valley fold both sides.

29. Outside reverse fold.

30. Pleat folds.

31. Outside reverse folds.

32. Completed Part One.

PART TWO

1. Valley fold and unfold.

2. Valley fold.

3. Valley fold and unfold.

4. Valley fold and unfold.

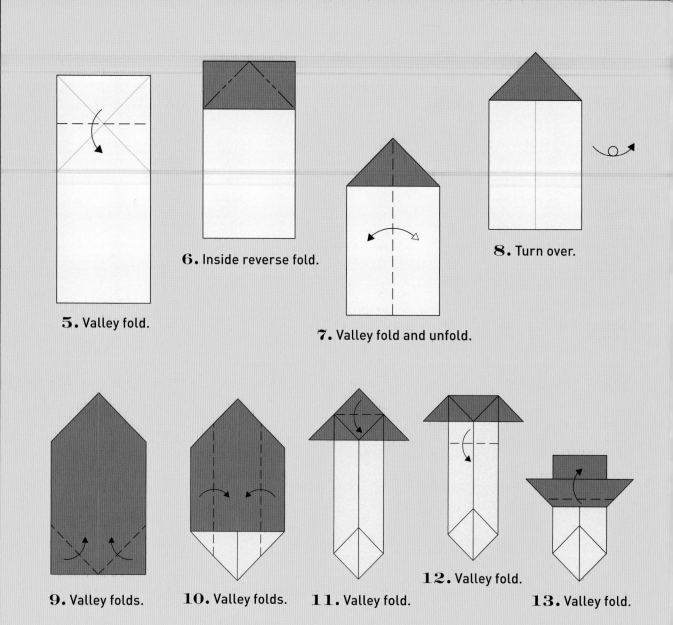

5. Valley fold.

6. Inside reverse fold.

7. Valley fold and unfold.

8. Turn over.

9. Valley folds.

10. Valley folds.

11. Valley fold.

12. Valley fold.

13. Valley fold.

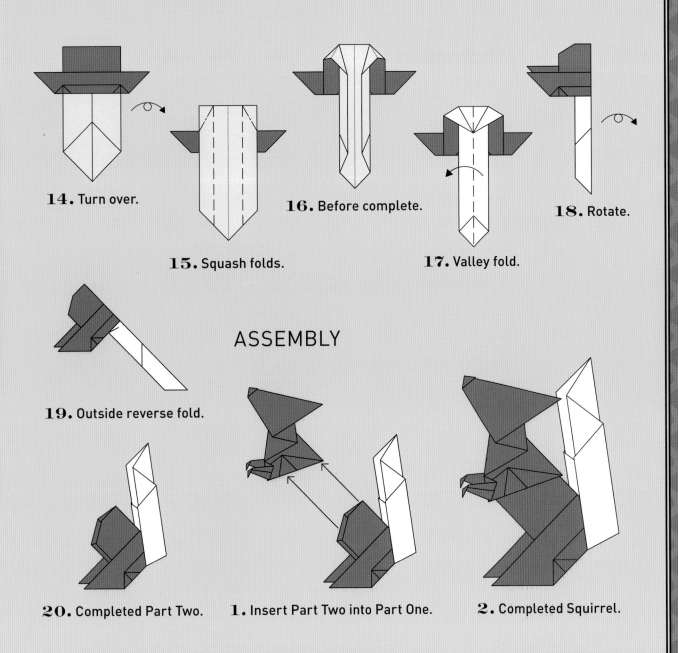

14. Turn over.

15. Squash folds.

16. Before complete.

17. Valley fold.

18. Rotate.

19. Outside reverse fold.

ASSEMBLY

20. Completed Part Two.

1. Insert Part Two into Part One.

2. Completed Squirrel.

CAMEL

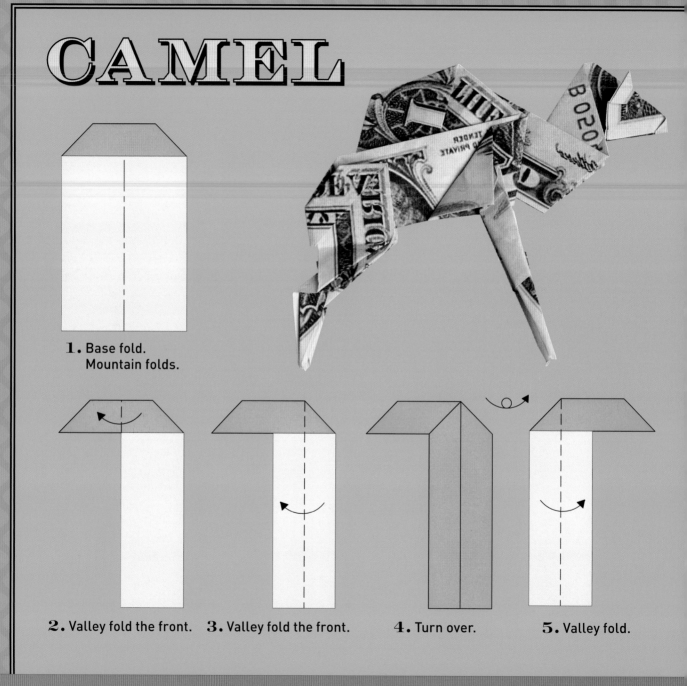

1. Base fold.
   Mountain folds.

2. Valley fold the front.

3. Valley fold the front.

4. Turn over.

5. Valley fold.

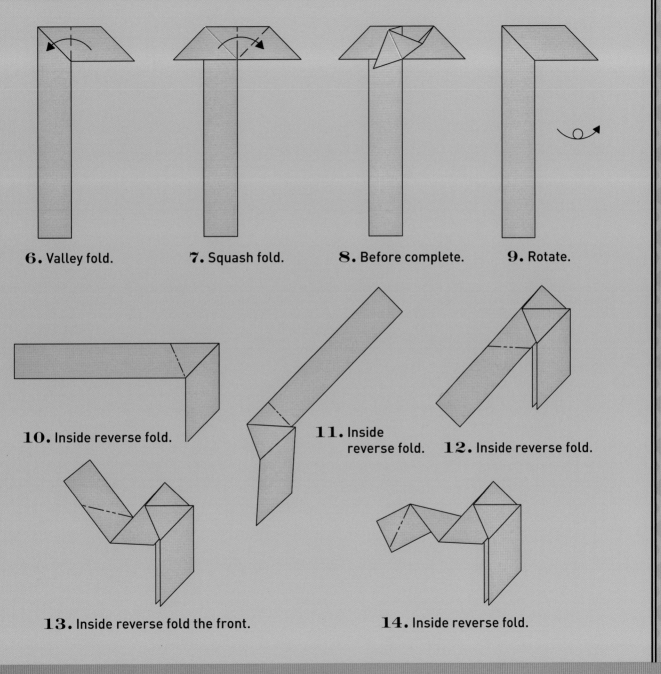

6. Valley fold.

7. Squash fold.

8. Before complete.

9. Rotate.

10. Inside reverse fold.

11. Inside reverse fold.

12. Inside reverse fold.

13. Inside reverse fold the front.

14. Inside reverse fold.

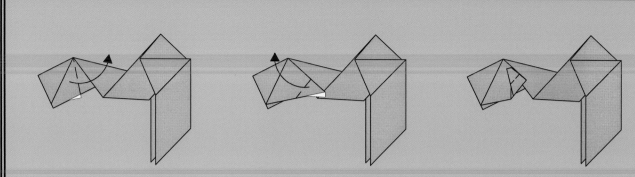

15. Valley fold the front.

16. Valley fold.

17. Valley fold.

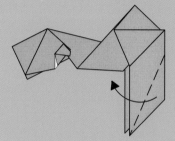

18. Valley fold the front.

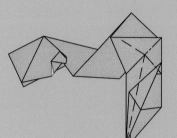

19. Squash fold.

20. Before complete.

21. Turn over.

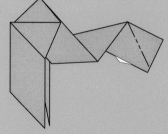

22. Inside reverse fold.

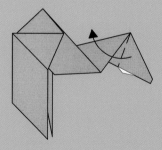

23. Valley fold.

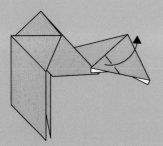

24. Valley fold.

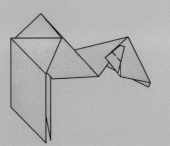

25. Valley fold.

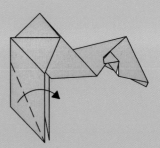

26. Valley fold.

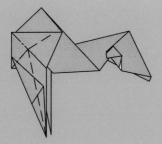

27. Squash fold.

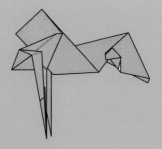

28. Before complete.

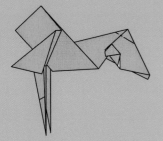

29. Mountain fold the front.

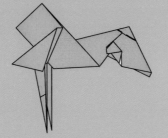

30. Valley fold and tuck in.

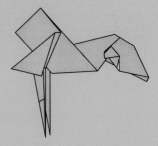

31. Completed Part One.

PART TWO

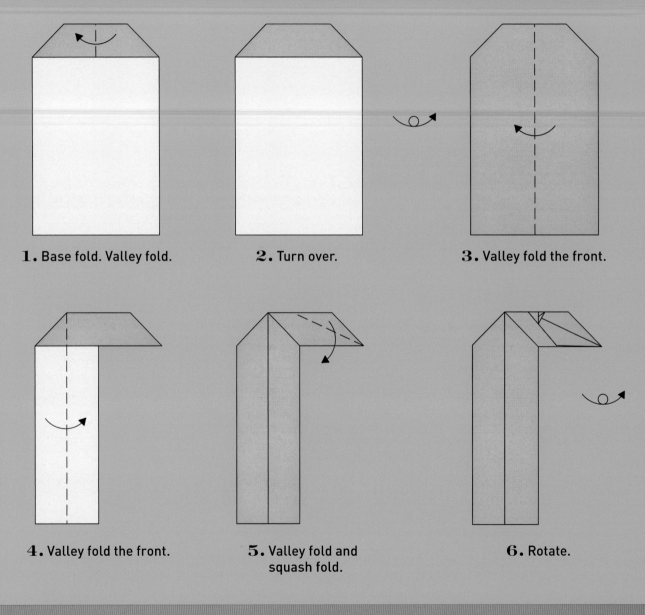

1. Base fold. Valley fold.

2. Turn over.

3. Valley fold the front.

4. Valley fold the front.

5. Valley fold and squash fold.

6. Rotate.

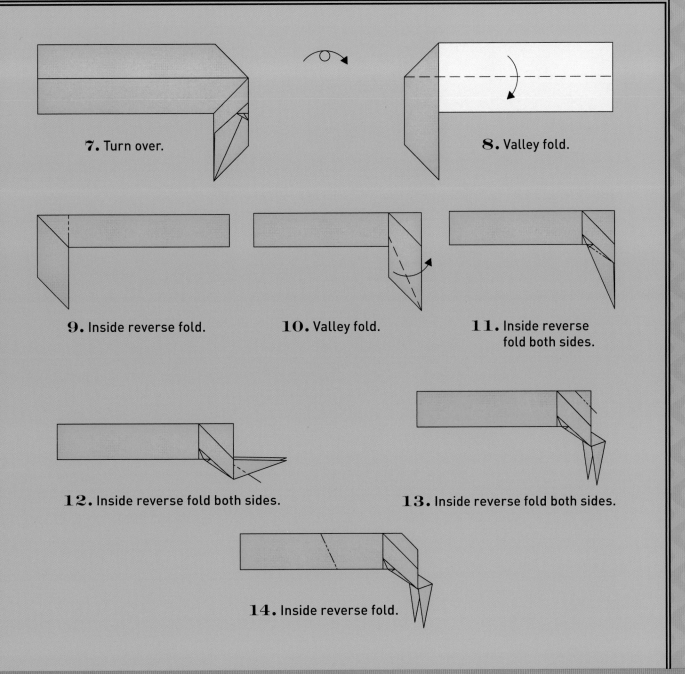

7. Turn over.

8. Valley fold.

9. Inside reverse fold.

10. Valley fold.

11. Inside reverse fold both sides.

12. Inside reverse fold both sides.

13. Inside reverse fold both sides.

14. Inside reverse fold.

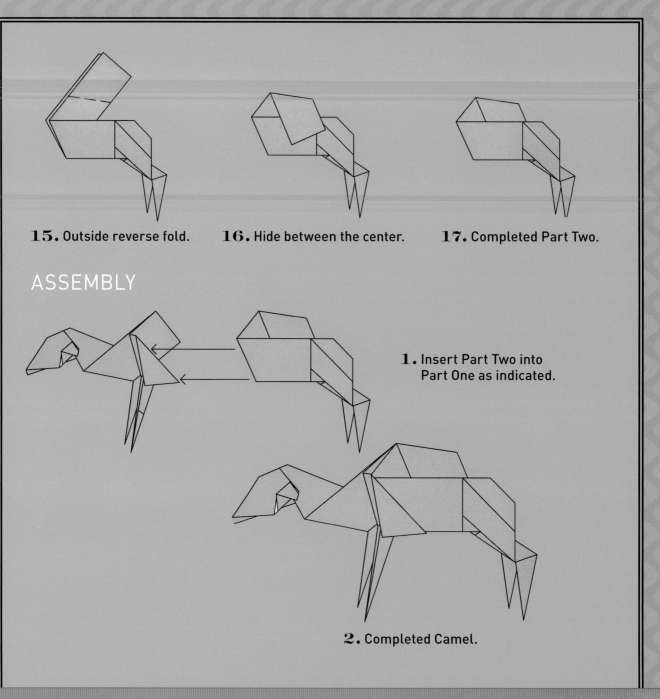

15. Outside reverse fold.

16. Hide between the center.

17. Completed Part Two.

ASSEMBLY

1. Insert Part Two into Part One as indicated.

2. Completed Camel.

GODZILLA

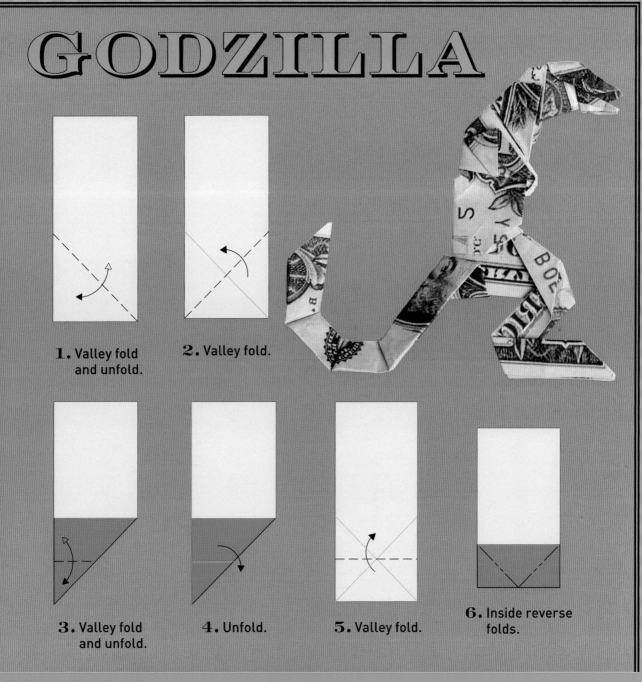

1. Valley fold and unfold.

2. Valley fold.

3. Valley fold and unfold.

4. Unfold.

5. Valley fold.

6. Inside reverse folds.

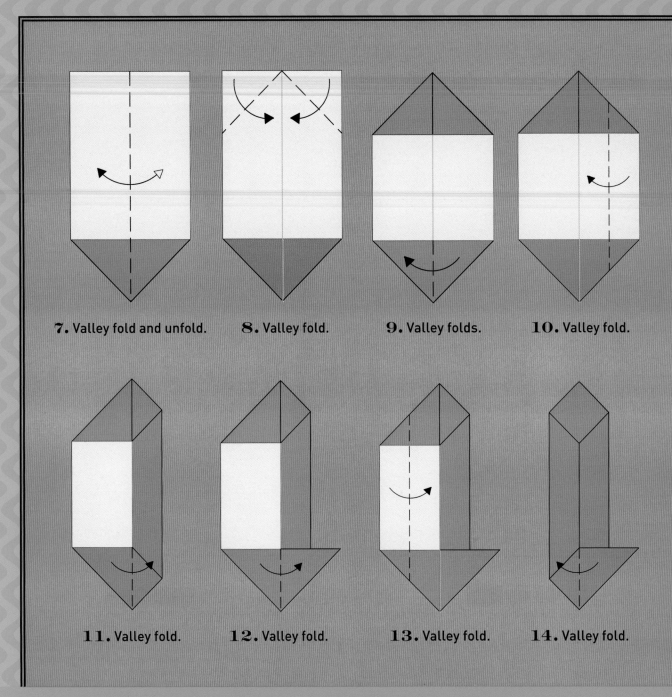

7. Valley fold and unfold.

8. Valley fold.

9. Valley folds.

10. Valley fold.

11. Valley fold.

12. Valley fold.

13. Valley fold.

14. Valley fold.

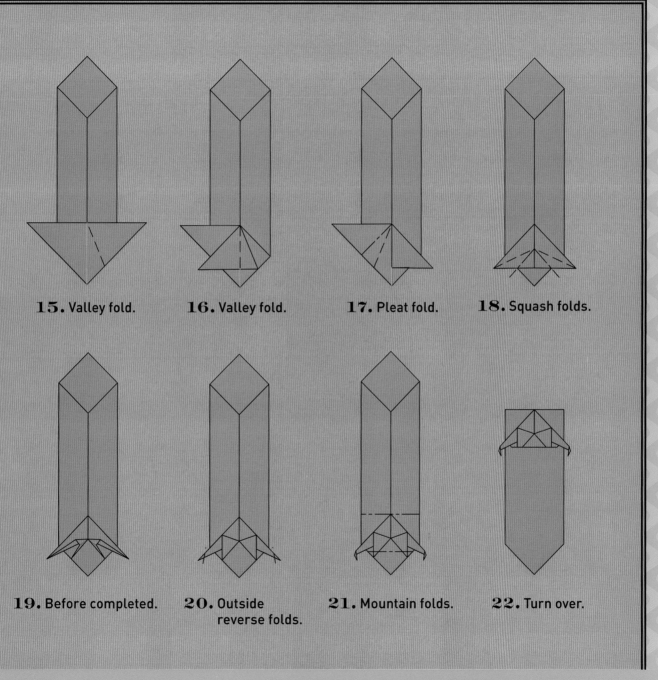

15. Valley fold.

16. Valley fold.

17. Pleat fold.

18. Squash folds.

19. Before completed.

20. Outside reverse folds.

21. Mountain folds.

22. Turn over.

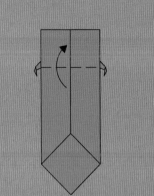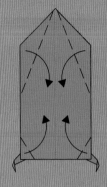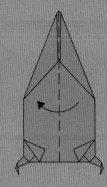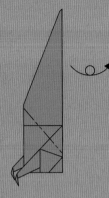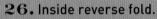

23. Valley fold. **24.** Valley folds. **25.** Valley fold. **26.** Inside reverse fold.

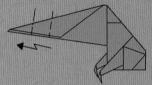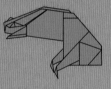

27. Crimp fold. **28.** Pleat fold both sides. **29.** Mountain folds. **30.** Completed Part One.

PART TWO

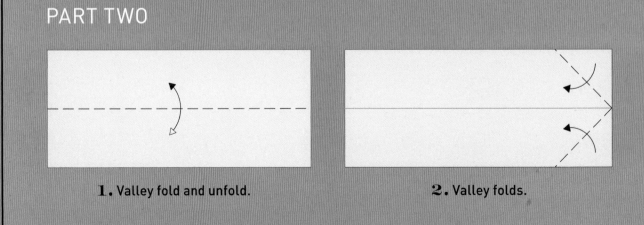

1. Valley fold and unfold. **2.** Valley folds.

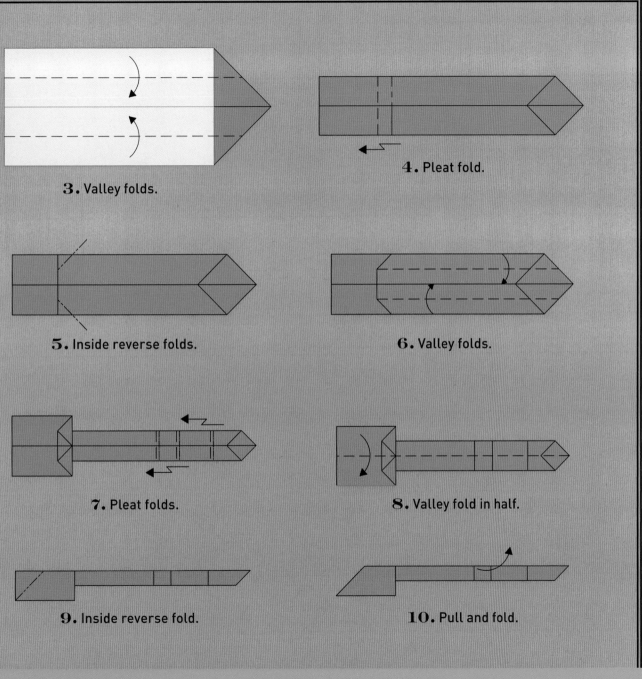

3. Valley folds.

4. Pleat fold.

5. Inside reverse folds.

6. Valley folds.

7. Pleat folds.

8. Valley fold in half.

9. Inside reverse fold.

10. Pull and fold.

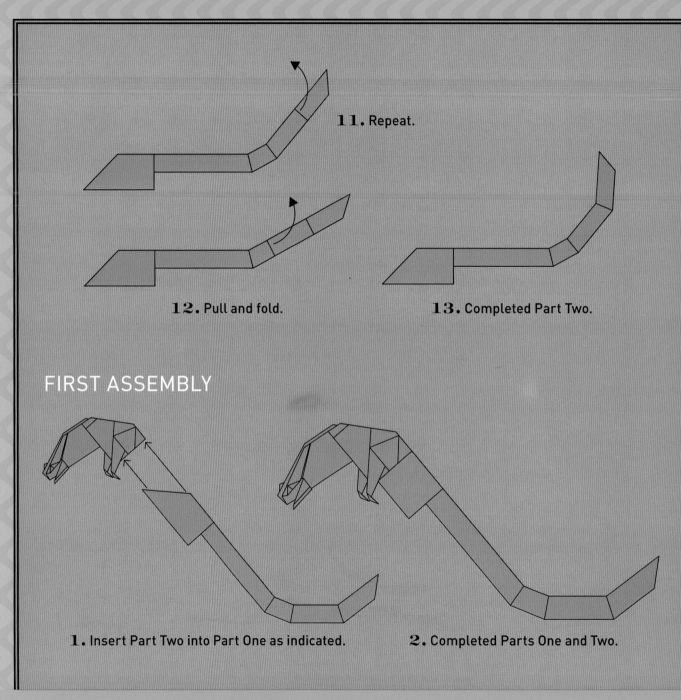

11. Repeat.

12. Pull and fold.

13. Completed Part Two.

FIRST ASSEMBLY

1. Insert Part Two into Part One as indicated.

2. Completed Parts One and Two.

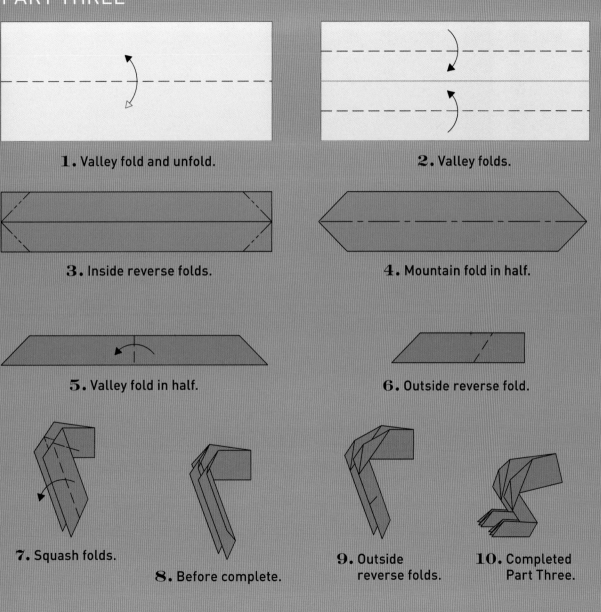

PART THREE

1. Valley fold and unfold.

2. Valley folds.

3. Inside reverse folds.

4. Mountain fold in half.

5. Valley fold in half.

6. Outside reverse fold.

7. Squash folds.

8. Before complete.

9. Outside reverse folds.

10. Completed Part Three.

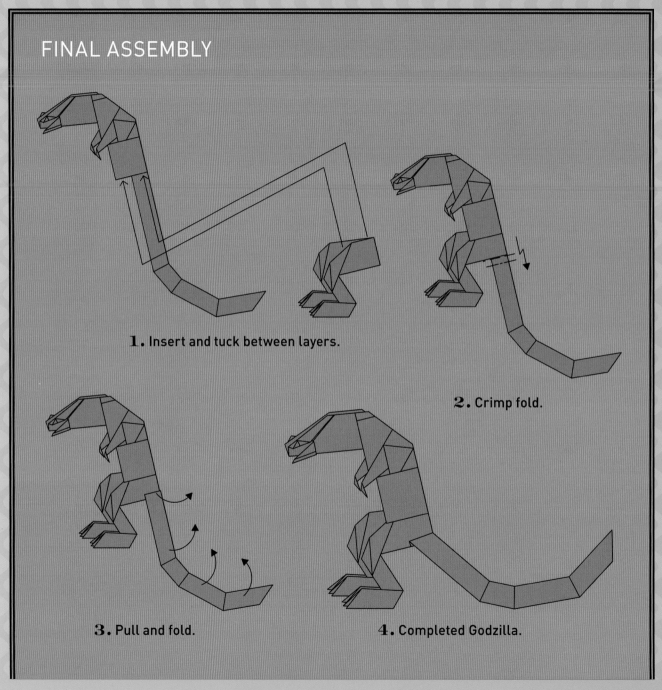

1. Insert and tuck between layers.

2. Crimp fold.

3. Pull and fold.

4. Completed Godzilla.

OSTRICH

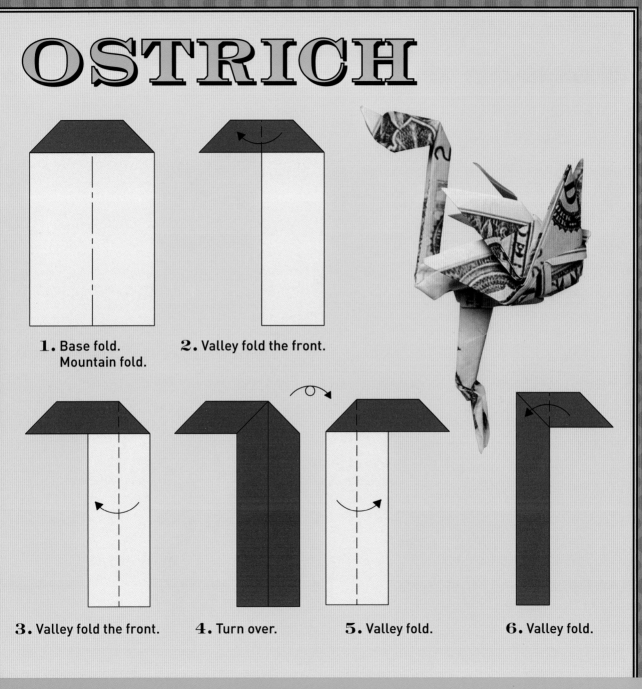

1. Base fold. Mountain fold.

2. Valley fold the front.

3. Valley fold the front.

4. Turn over.

5. Valley fold.

6. Valley fold.

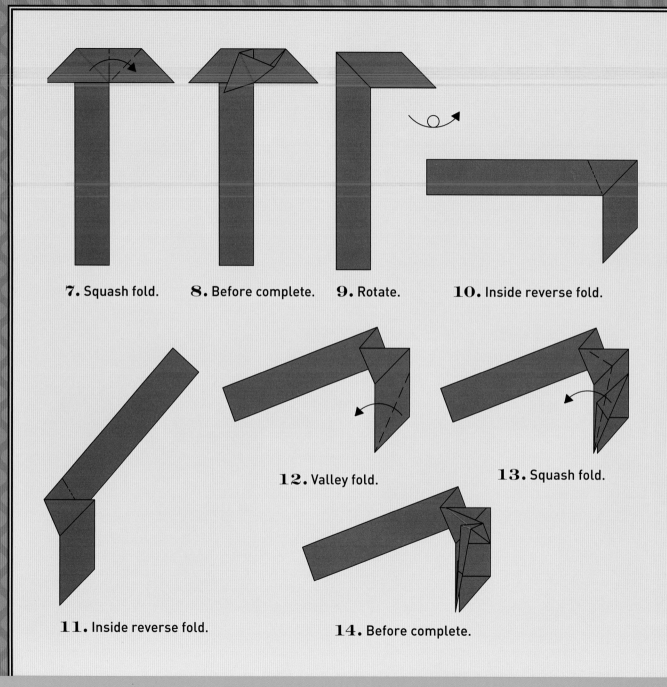

7. Squash fold.

8. Before complete.

9. Rotate.

10. Inside reverse fold.

12. Valley fold.

13. Squash fold.

11. Inside reverse fold.

14. Before complete.

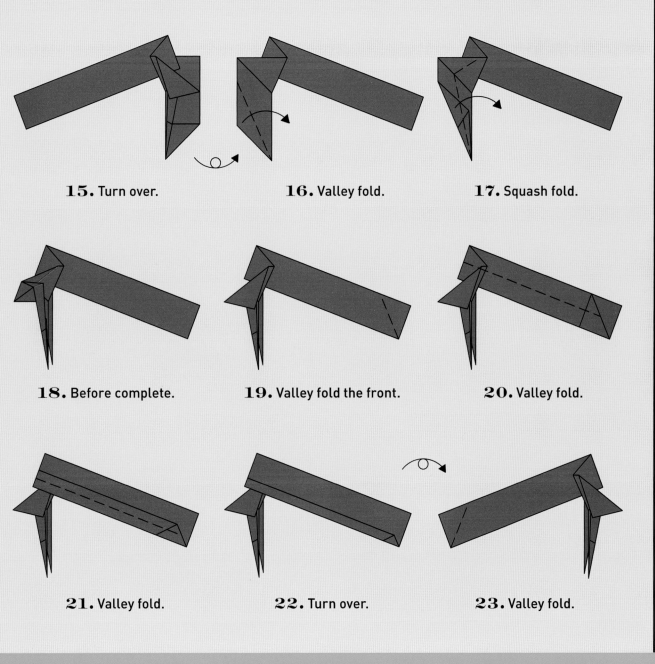

15. Turn over.

16. Valley fold.

17. Squash fold.

18. Before complete.

19. Valley fold the front.

20. Valley fold.

21. Valley fold.

22. Turn over.

23. Valley fold.

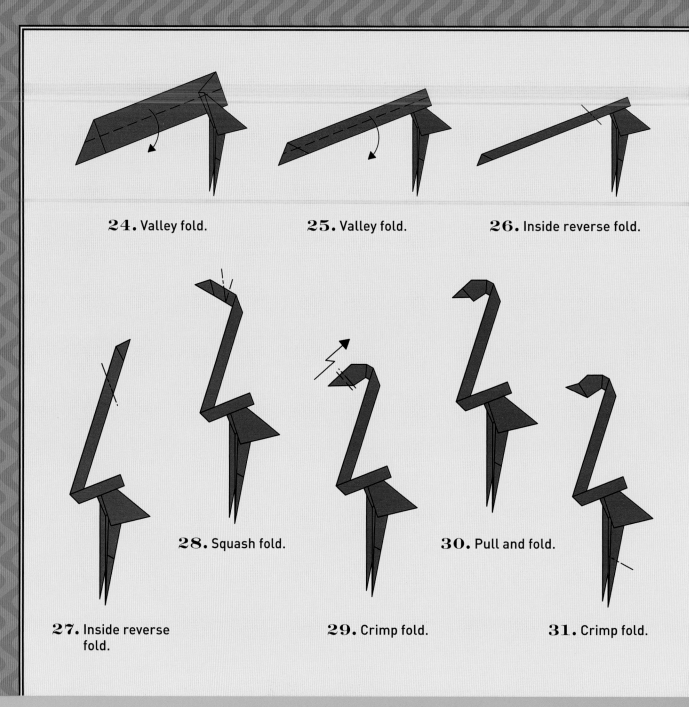

24. Valley fold.

25. Valley fold.

26. Inside reverse fold.

28. Squash fold.

30. Pull and fold.

27. Inside reverse fold.

29. Crimp fold.

31. Crimp fold.

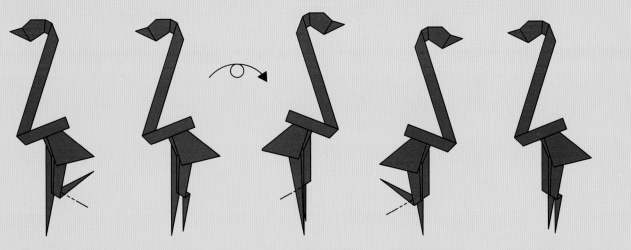

32. Inside reverse fold.

33. Turn over.

34. Inside reverse fold.

35. Repeat.

36. Completed Part One.

PART TWO

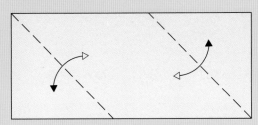

1. Valley folds and unfold.

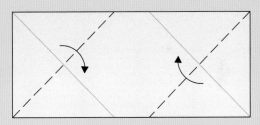

2. Valley folds.

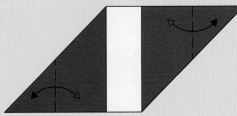

3. Valley folds and unfold.

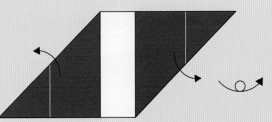

4. Valley fold to unfold and rotate.

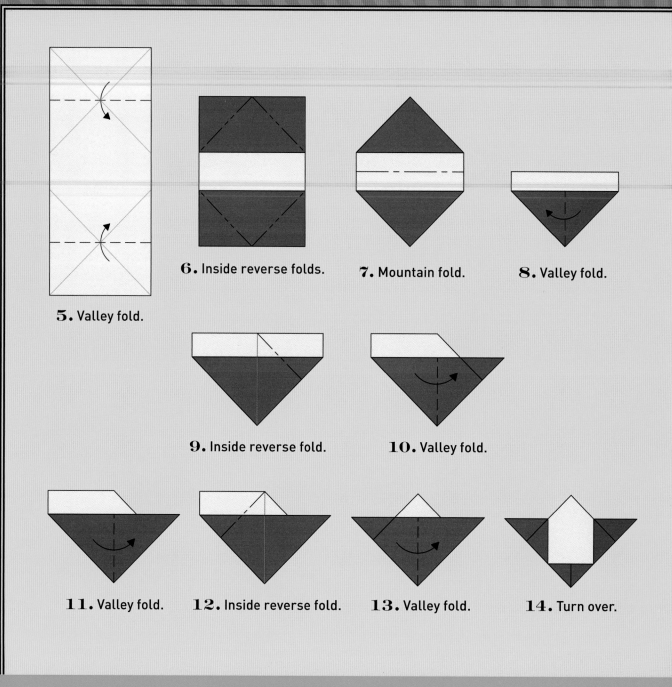

5. Valley fold.

6. Inside reverse folds.

7. Mountain fold.

8. Valley fold.

9. Inside reverse fold.

10. Valley fold.

11. Valley fold.

12. Inside reverse fold.

13. Valley fold.

14. Turn over.

15. Valley fold.

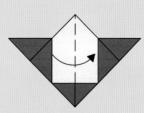

16. Valley fold.

17. Valley fold.

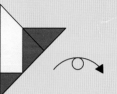

18. Rotate.

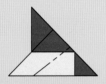

19. Inside reverse fold.

20. Squash fold.

21. Before complete.

22. Completed Part Two.

ASSEMBLY

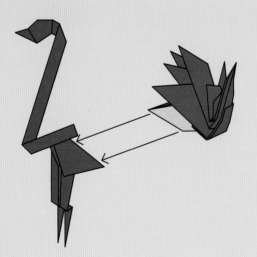

1. Insert Part Two into Part One as indicated.

2. Completed Ostrich.

KING
COBRA

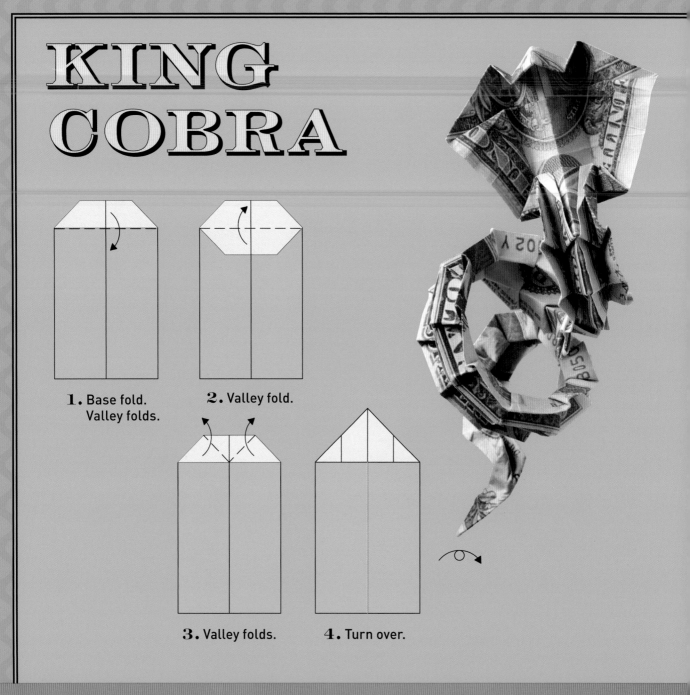

1. Base fold. Valley folds.

2. Valley fold.

3. Valley folds.

4. Turn over.

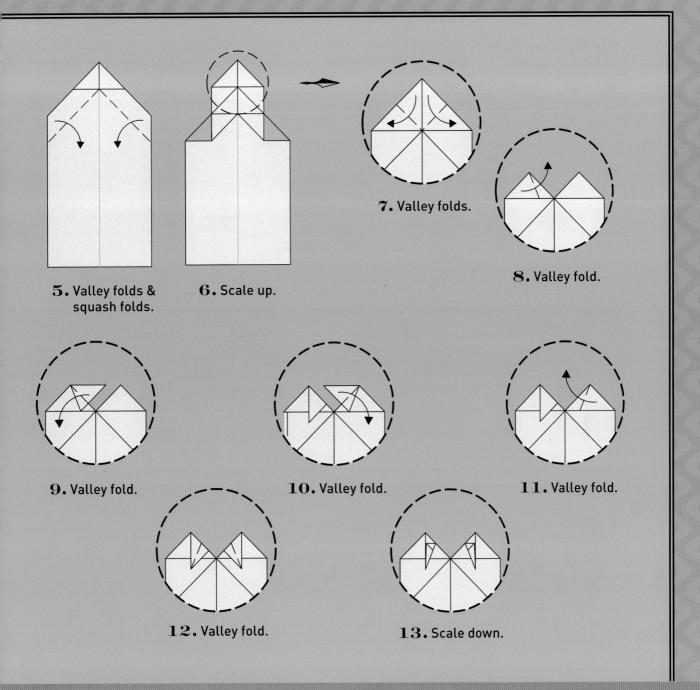

5. Valley folds & squash folds.

6. Scale up.

7. Valley folds.

8. Valley fold.

9. Valley fold.

10. Valley fold.

11. Valley fold.

12. Valley fold.

13. Scale down.

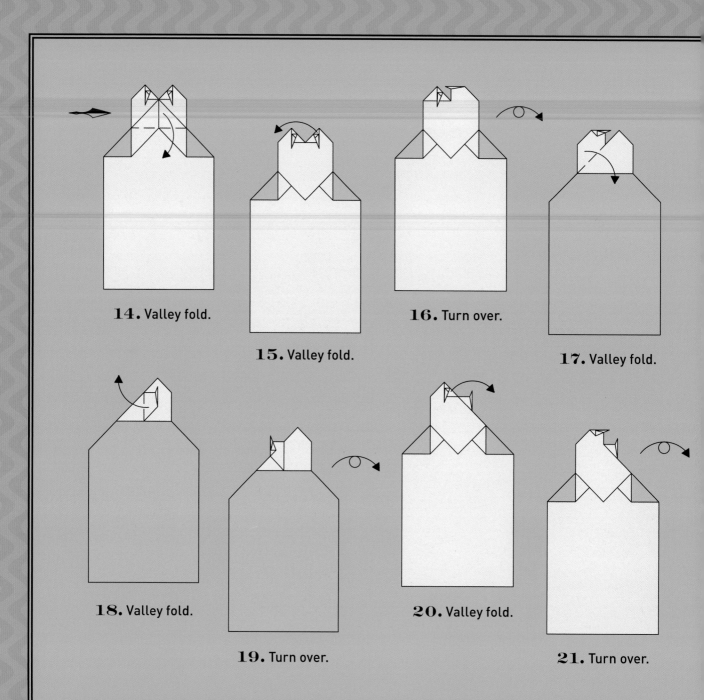

14. Valley fold.

15. Valley fold.

16. Turn over.

17. Valley fold.

18. Valley fold.

19. Turn over.

20. Valley fold.

21. Turn over.

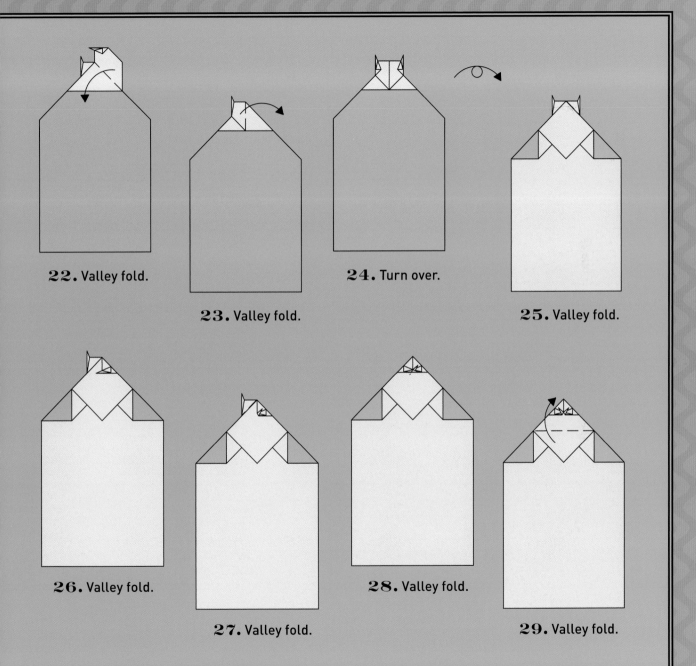

22. Valley fold.

23. Valley fold.

24. Turn over.

25. Valley fold.

26. Valley fold.

27. Valley fold.

28. Valley fold.

29. Valley fold.

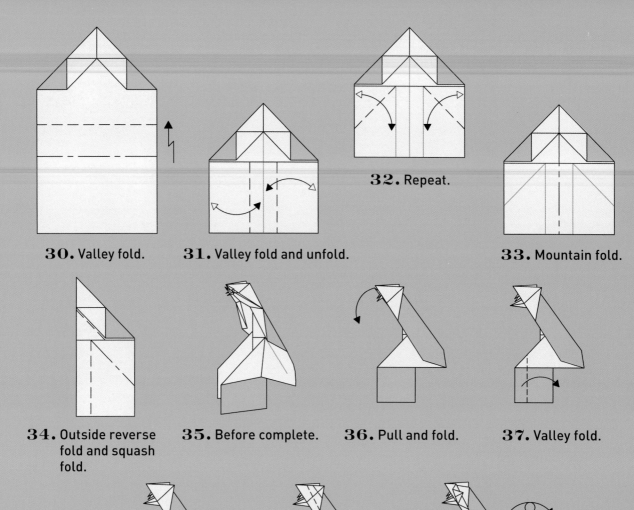

30. Valley fold.

31. Valley fold and unfold.

32. Repeat.

33. Mountain fold.

34. Outside reverse fold and squash fold.

35. Before complete.

36. Pull and fold.

37. Valley fold.

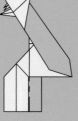

38. Valley fold.

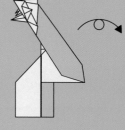

39. Pleat fold.

40. Turn over.

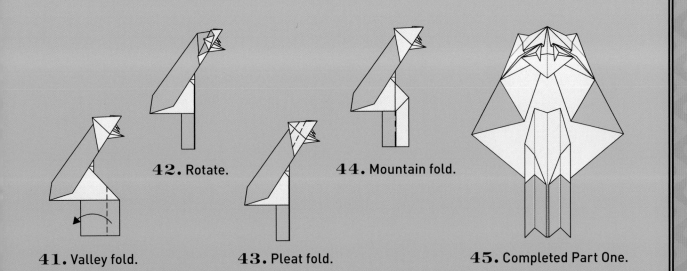

41. Valley fold.

42. Rotate.

43. Pleat fold.

44. Mountain fold.

45. Completed Part One.

PART TWO

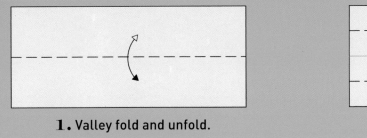

1. Valley fold and unfold.

2. Valley fold.

3. Mountain folds and unfold.

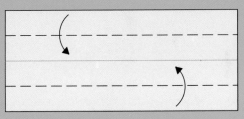

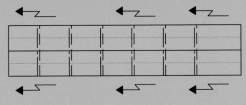

4. Pleat folds.

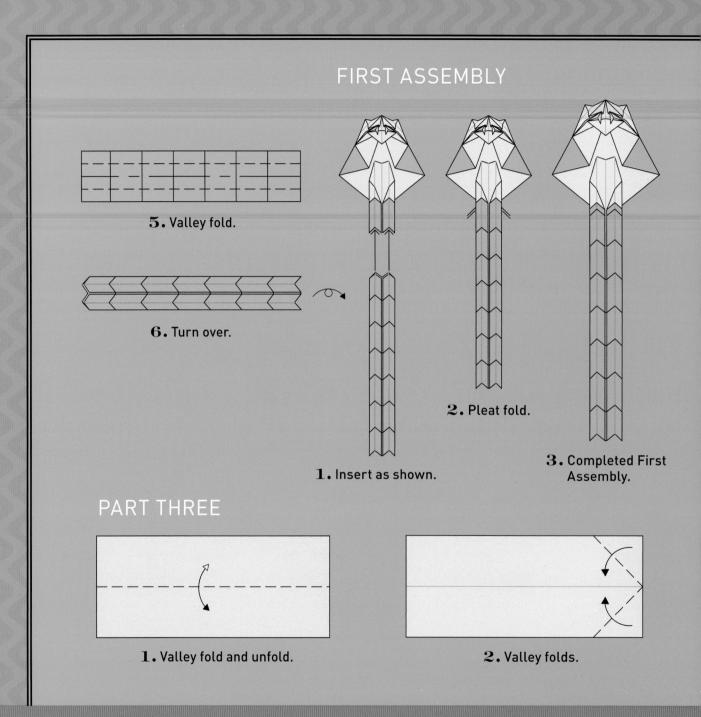

5. Valley fold.

6. Turn over.

1. Insert as shown.

2. Pleat fold.

3. Completed First Assembly.

PART THREE

1. Valley fold and unfold.

2. Valley folds.

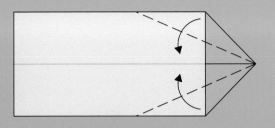

3. Valley folds.

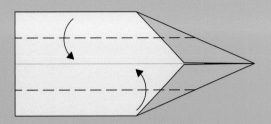

4. Valley folds.

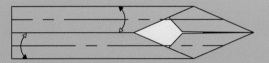

5. Valley folds and unfold.

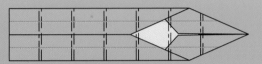

6. Pleat folds.

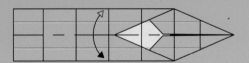

7. Mountain fold and unfold.

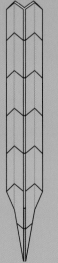

9. Completed Part Three.

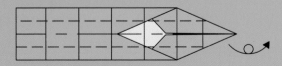

8. Pleat fold, rotate, and turn over.

FINAL ASSEMBLY

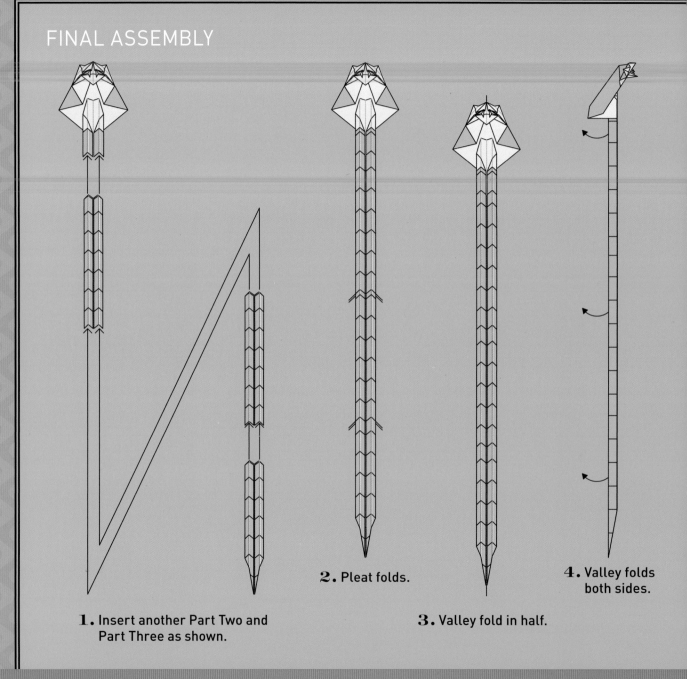

1. Insert another Part Two and Part Three as shown.

2. Pleat folds.

3. Valley fold in half.

4. Valley folds both sides.

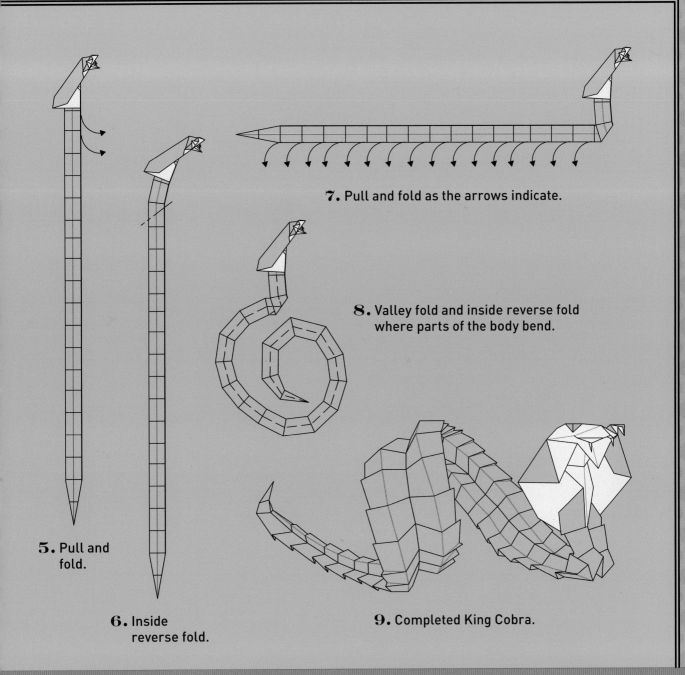

5. Pull and fold.

6. Inside reverse fold.

7. Pull and fold as the arrows indicate.

8. Valley fold and inside reverse fold where parts of the body bend.

9. Completed King Cobra.

MOOSE

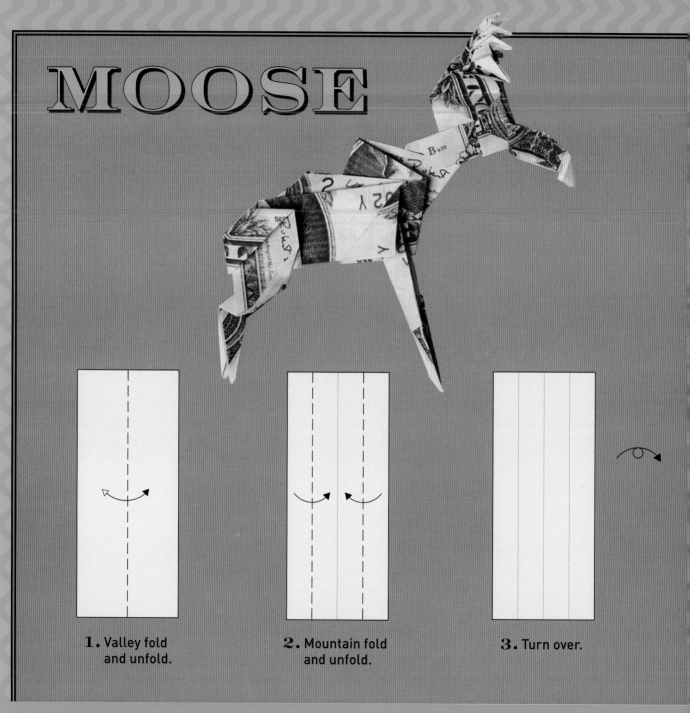

1. Valley fold and unfold.

2. Mountain fold and unfold.

3. Turn over.

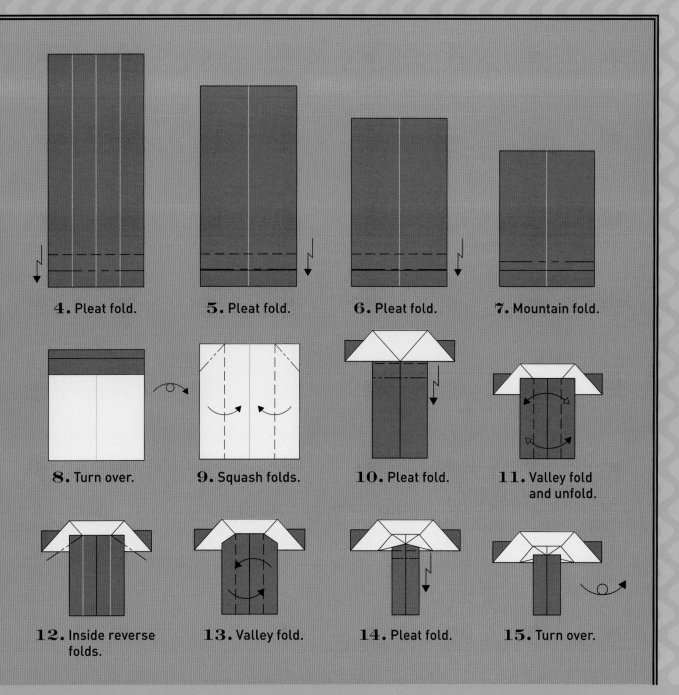

4. Pleat fold.

5. Pleat fold.

6. Pleat fold.

7. Mountain fold.

8. Turn over.

9. Squash folds.

10. Pleat fold.

11. Valley fold and unfold.

12. Inside reverse folds.

13. Valley fold.

14. Pleat fold.

15. Turn over.

MOOSE

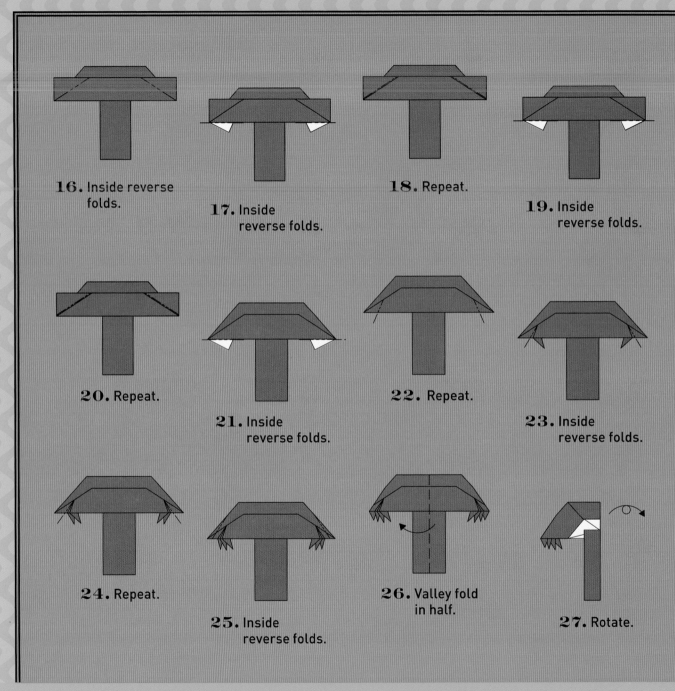

16. Inside reverse folds.

17. Inside reverse folds.

18. Repeat.

19. Inside reverse folds.

20. Repeat.

21. Inside reverse folds.

22. Repeat.

23. Inside reverse folds.

24. Repeat.

25. Inside reverse folds.

26. Valley fold in half.

27. Rotate.

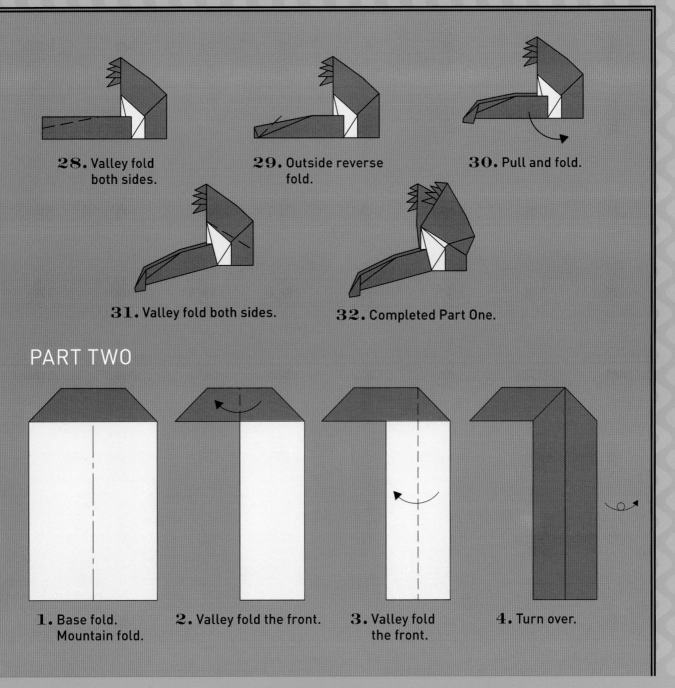

28. Valley fold both sides.

29. Outside reverse fold.

30. Pull and fold.

31. Valley fold both sides.

32. Completed Part One.

PART TWO

1. Base fold. Mountain fold.

2. Valley fold the front.

3. Valley fold the front.

4. Turn over.

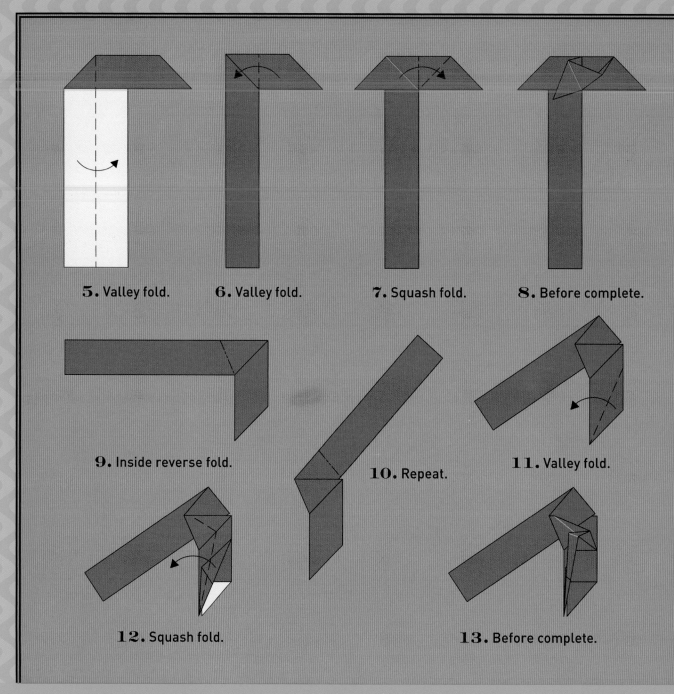

5. Valley fold.

6. Valley fold.

7. Squash fold.

8. Before complete.

9. Inside reverse fold.

10. Repeat.

11. Valley fold.

12. Squash fold.

13. Before complete.

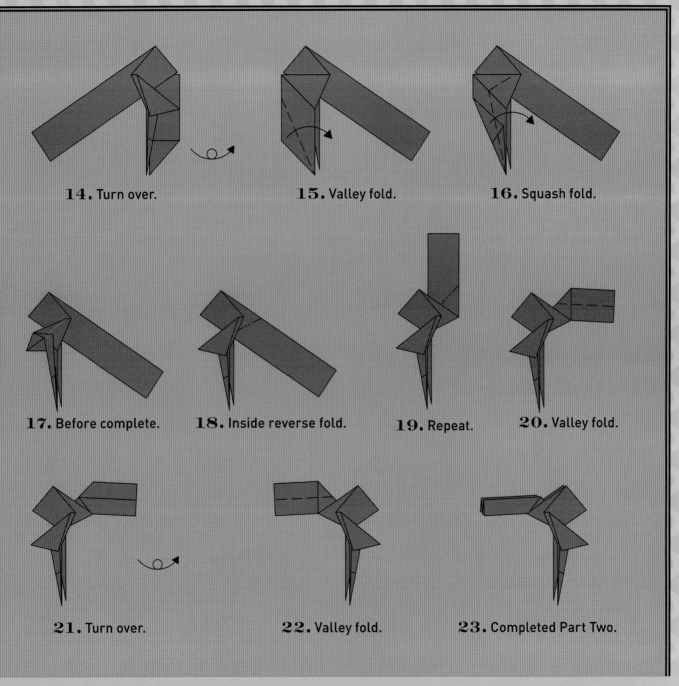

14. Turn over.

15. Valley fold.

16. Squash fold.

17. Before complete.

18. Inside reverse fold.

19. Repeat.

20. Valley fold.

21. Turn over.

22. Valley fold.

23. Completed Part Two.

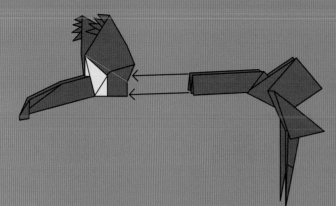

1. Insert Part Two into Part One as indicated.

2. Completed First Assembly.

PART THREE

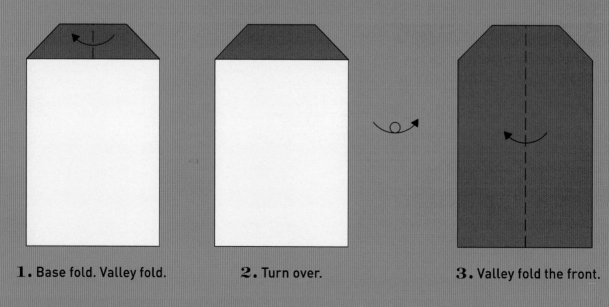

1. Base fold. Valley fold.

2. Turn over.

3. Valley fold the front.

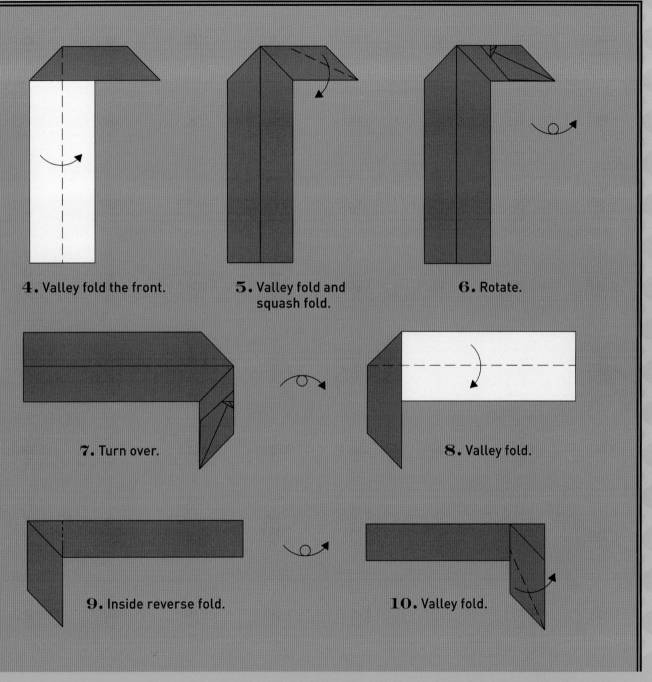

4. Valley fold the front.

5. Valley fold and squash fold.

6. Rotate.

7. Turn over.

8. Valley fold.

9. Inside reverse fold.

10. Valley fold.

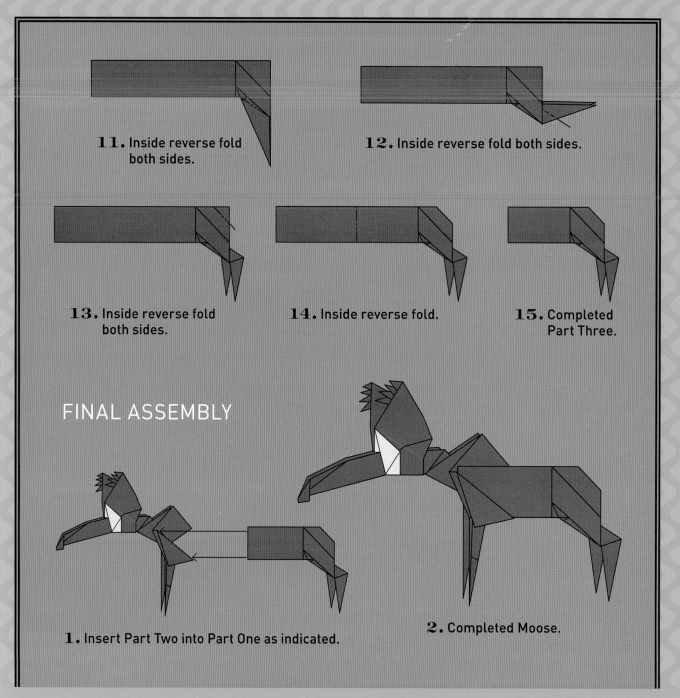

11. Inside reverse fold both sides.

12. Inside reverse fold both sides.

13. Inside reverse fold both sides.

14. Inside reverse fold.

15. Completed Part Three.

FINAL ASSEMBLY

1. Insert Part Two into Part One as indicated.

2. Completed Moose.

CENTIPEDE

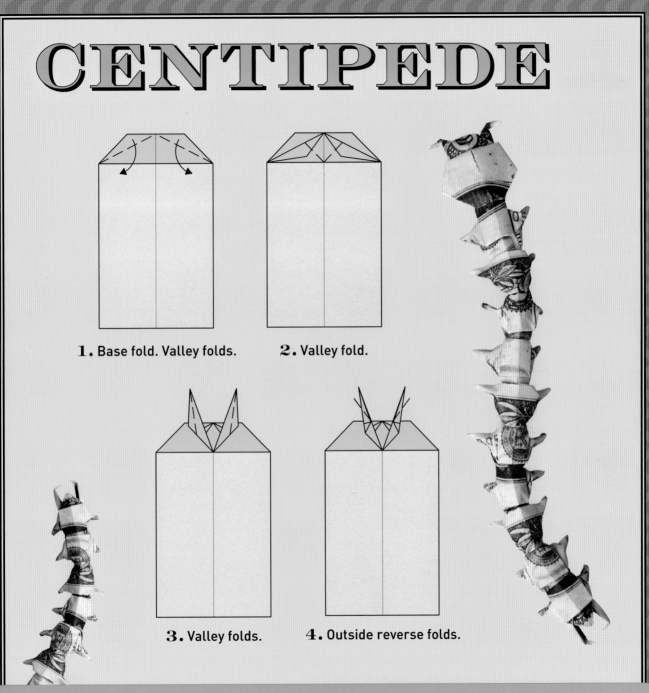

1. Base fold. Valley folds.

2. Valley fold.

3. Valley folds.

4. Outside reverse folds.

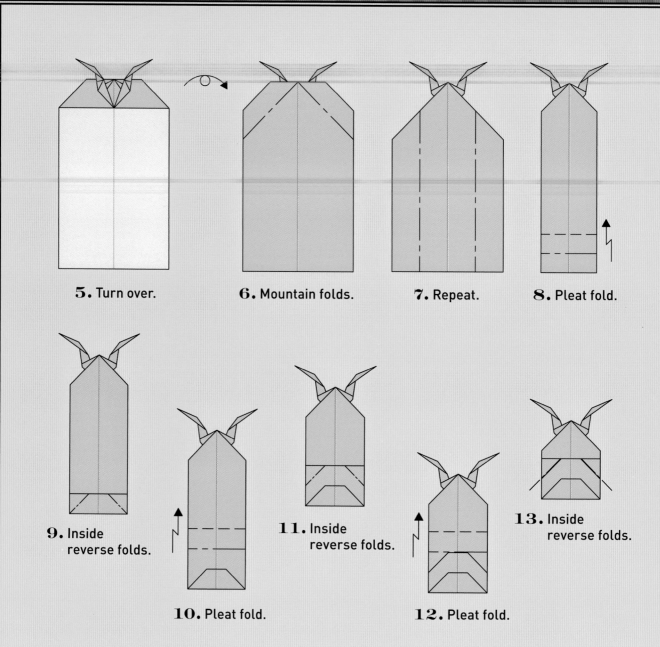

5. Turn over.

6. Mountain folds.

7. Repeat.

8. Pleat fold.

9. Inside reverse folds.

10. Pleat fold.

11. Inside reverse folds.

12. Pleat fold.

13. Inside reverse folds.

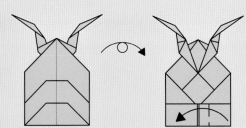

14. Turn over.

15. Valley fold.

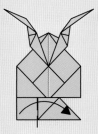

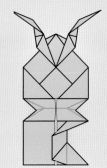

16. Before complete.

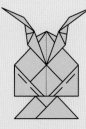

17. Valley fold.

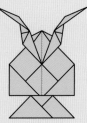

18. Before complete.

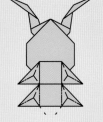

19. Hide behind.

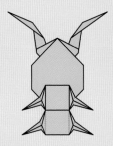

20. Valley folds.

21. Valley folds.

22. Turn over.

23. Pinch and fold.

24. Completed Part One.

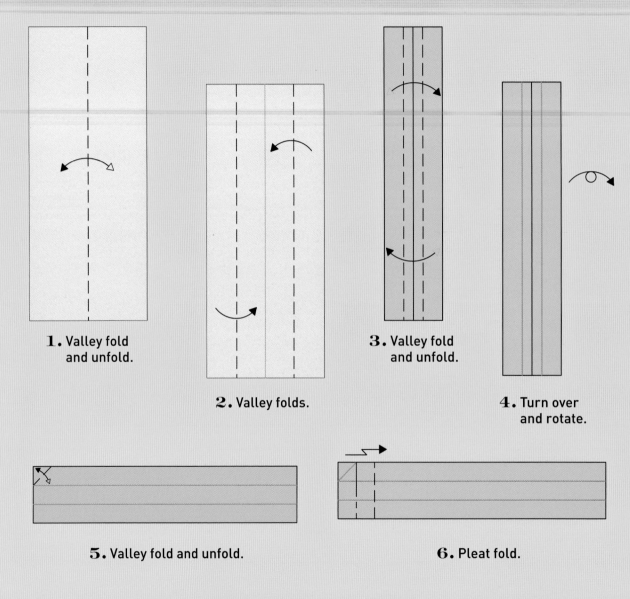

1. Valley fold and unfold.

2. Valley folds.

3. Valley fold and unfold.

4. Turn over and rotate.

5. Valley fold and unfold.

6. Pleat fold.

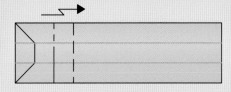

8. Pleat fold.

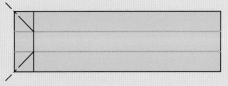

7. Inside reverse folds.

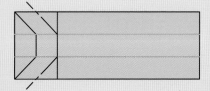

9. Inside reverse folds.

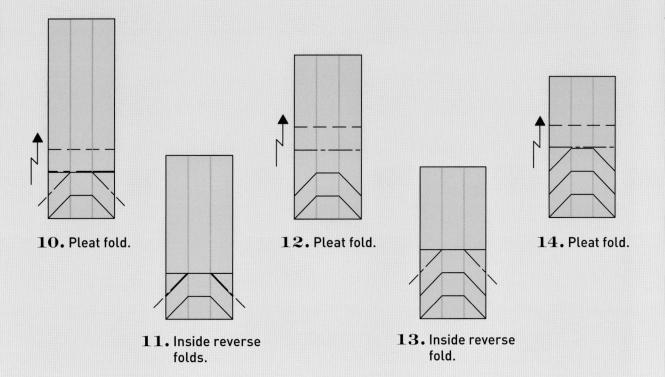

10. Pleat fold.

11. Inside reverse folds.

12. Pleat fold.

13. Inside reverse fold.

14. Pleat fold.

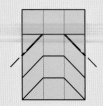

15. Inside reverse folds.

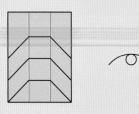

16. Turn over.

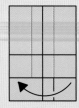

17. Valley fold.

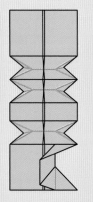

18. Before complete.

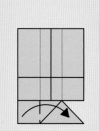

19. Valley fold.

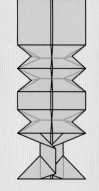

20. Before complete.

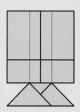

21. Hide behind.

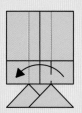

22. Valley fold.

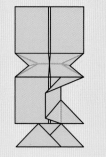

23. Before complete.

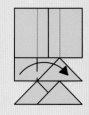

24. Valley fold.

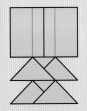

25. Hide behind.

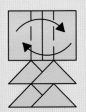

26. Valley folds.

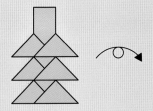

27. Turn over.

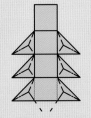

28. Pinch and fold.

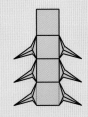

29. Completed Part Two.

FIRST ASSEMBLY

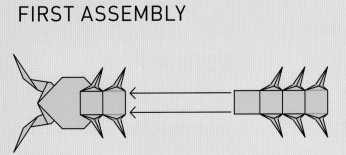

1. Insert as shown.

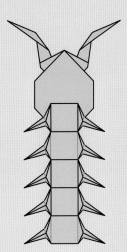

NOTICE:
Make another
Part Two for the
Final Assembly.

2. Completed First Assembly.

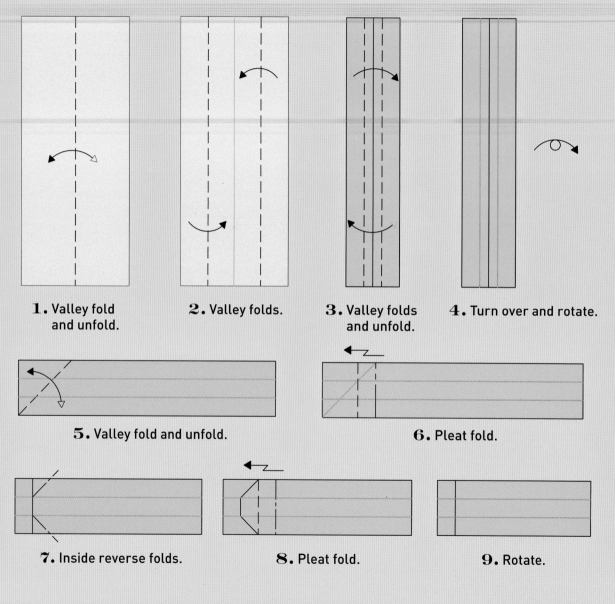

1. Valley fold and unfold.

2. Valley folds.

3. Valley folds and unfold.

4. Turn over and rotate.

5. Valley fold and unfold.

6. Pleat fold.

7. Inside reverse folds.

8. Pleat fold.

9. Rotate.

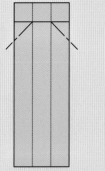

10. Inside reverse folds.

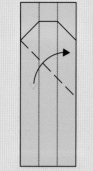

11. Valley fold and unfold.

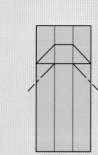

12. Pleat fold.

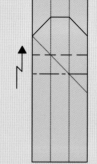

13. Inside reverse folds.

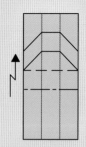

14. Pleat fold.

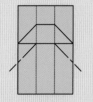

15. Inside reverse folds.

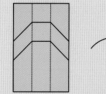

16. Turn over.

17. Valley fold.

18. Before complete.

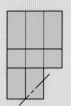

19. Inside reverse fold.

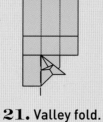

20. Valley fold.

21. Valley fold.

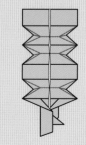

22. Before complete.

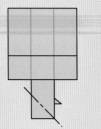

23. Inside reverse fold.

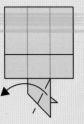

24. Valley fold.

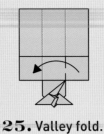

25. Valley fold.

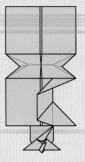

26. Before complete.

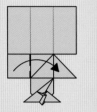

27. Valley fold.

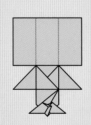

28. Tuck in.

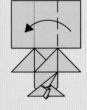
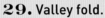

29. Valley fold.

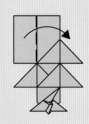

30. Valley fold.

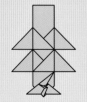

31. Tuck in.

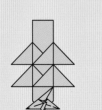

32. Valley folds.

33. Turn over.

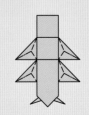

34. Pinch and fold.

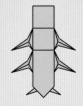

35. Completed Part Three.

FINAL ASSEMBLY

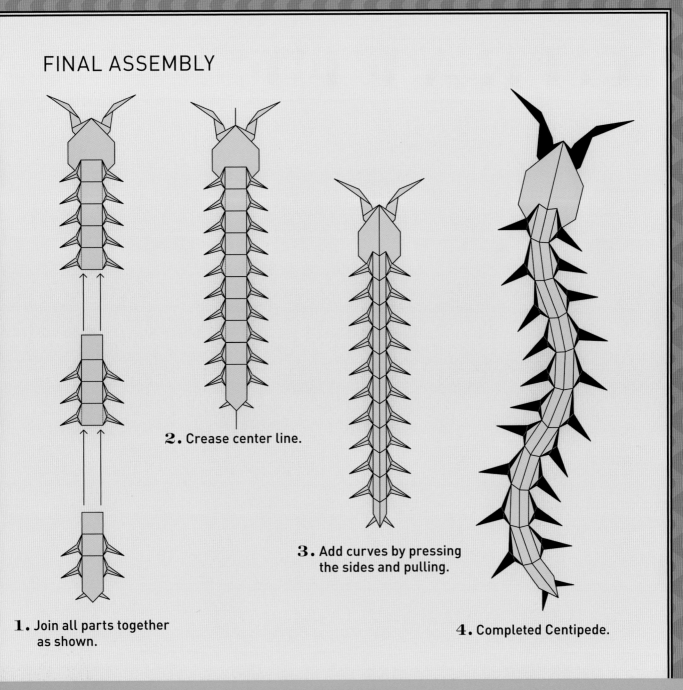

1. Join all parts together as shown.

2. Crease center line.

3. Add curves by pressing the sides and pulling.

4. Completed Centipede.

GIRAFFE

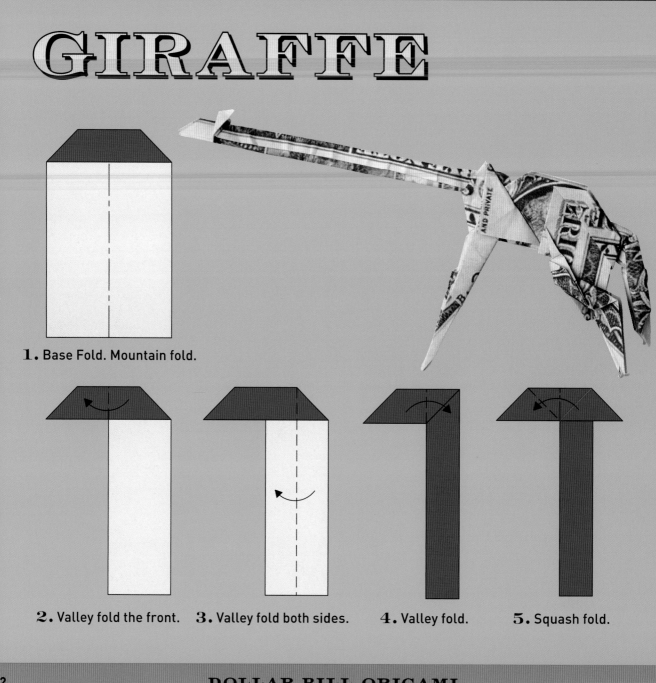

1. Base Fold. Mountain fold.

2. Valley fold the front.

3. Valley fold both sides.

4. Valley fold.

5. Squash fold.

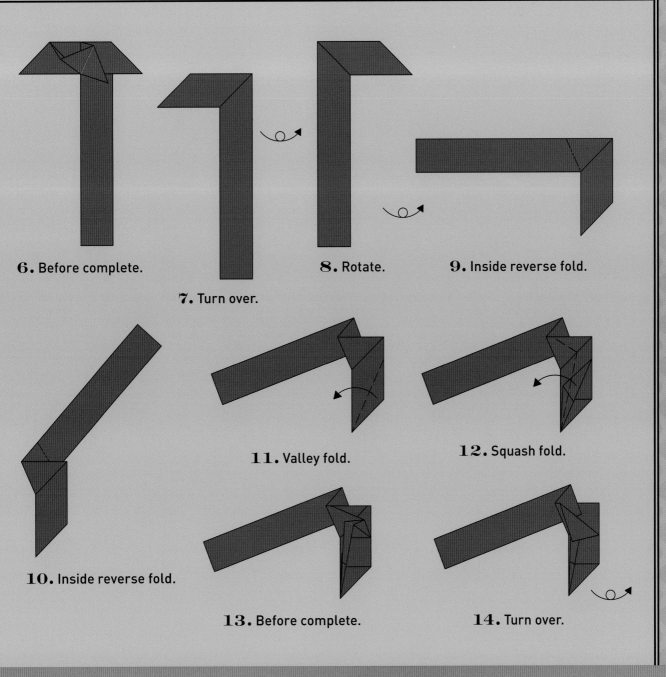

6. Before complete.

7. Turn over.

8. Rotate.

9. Inside reverse fold.

10. Inside reverse fold.

11. Valley fold.

12. Squash fold.

13. Before complete.

14. Turn over.

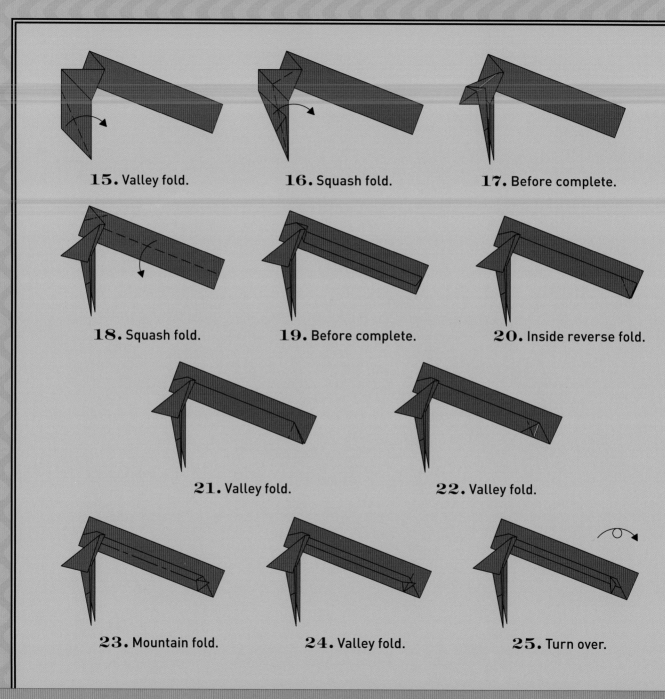

15. Valley fold.

16. Squash fold.

17. Before complete.

18. Squash fold.

19. Before complete.

20. Inside reverse fold.

21. Valley fold.

22. Valley fold.

23. Mountain fold.

24. Valley fold.

25. Turn over.

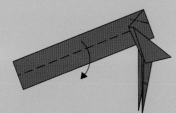

26. Squash fold.

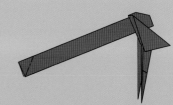

27. Before complete.

28. Inside reverse fold.

29. Valley fold.

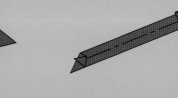

30. Valley fold.

31. Mountain fold.

32. Valley fold.

33. Valley folds to add curves.

34. Completed Part One.

PART TWO

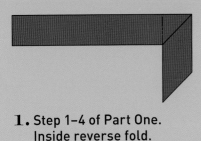

1. Step 1–4 of Part One.
Inside reverse fold.

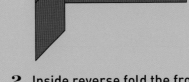

2. Inside reverse fold the front.

3. Valley fold the front.

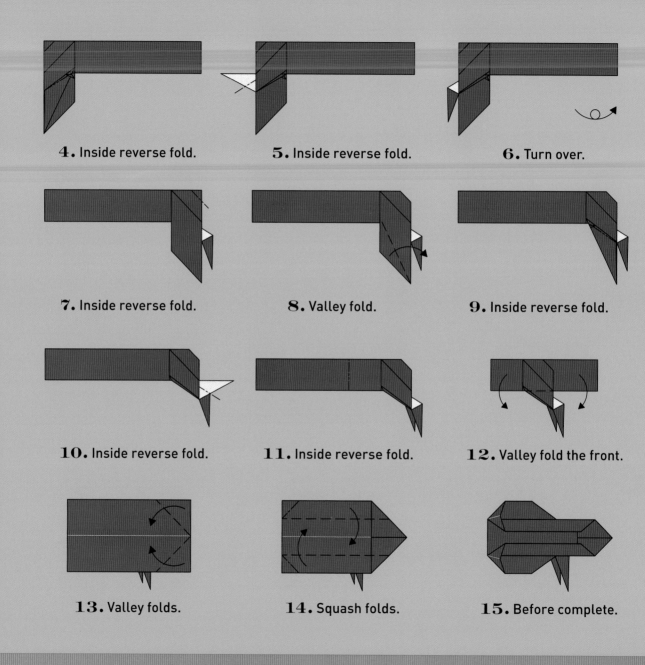

4. Inside reverse fold.

5. Inside reverse fold.

6. Turn over.

7. Inside reverse fold.

8. Valley fold.

9. Inside reverse fold.

10. Inside reverse fold.

11. Inside reverse fold.

12. Valley fold the front.

13. Valley folds.

14. Squash folds.

15. Before complete.

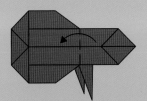 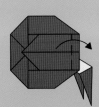 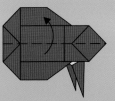 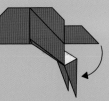

16. Valley fold. **17.** Valley fold. **18.** Valley fold. **19.** Pull and fold.

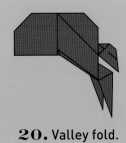 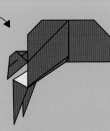 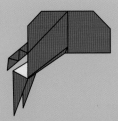

20. Valley fold. **21.** Turn over. **22.** Valley fold. **23.** Completed Part Two.

ASSEMBLY

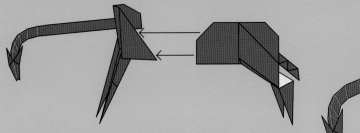

1. Insert in the direction of the arrows.

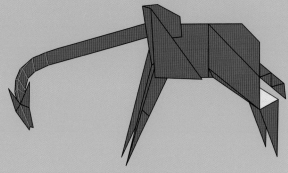

2. Completed Giraffe.

CHINESE DRAGON

1. Valley folds.

2. Valley fold and unfold.

3. Valley folds.

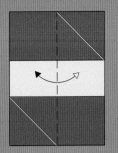

4. Valley fold and unfold.

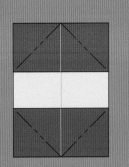

5. Inside reverse folds.

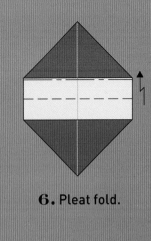

6. Pleat fold.

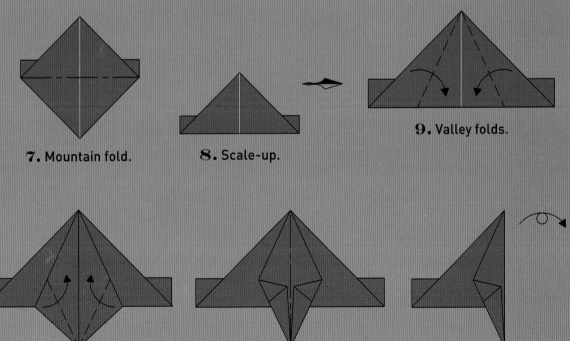

7. Mountain fold.

8. Scale-up.

9. Valley folds.

10. Valley folds.

11. Mountain fold in half.

12. Rotate.

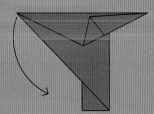

13. Pull and squash fold.

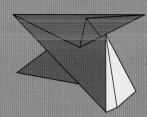

14. Before complete.

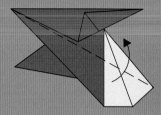

15. Valley fold.

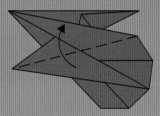

16. Valley fold.

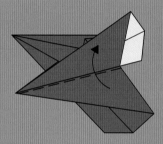

17. Valley fold the front.

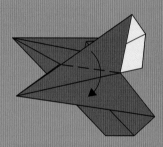

18. Valley fold.

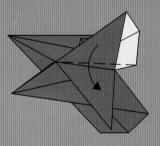

19. Valley fold.

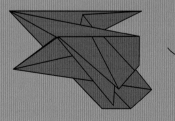
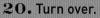

20. Turn over.

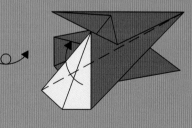

21. Valley fold.

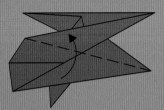

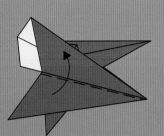

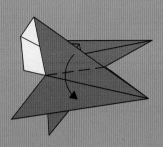

22. Valley fold.　　　　**23.** Valley fold the front.　　　　**24.** Valley fold.

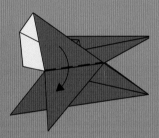

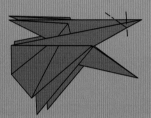

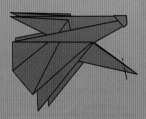

25. Valley fold.　　　　**26.** Squash fold.　　　　**27.** Inside reverse fold.

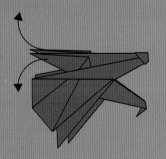

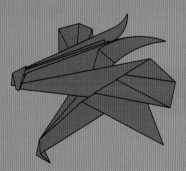

28. Pull and curl outward.

29. Completed Part One.

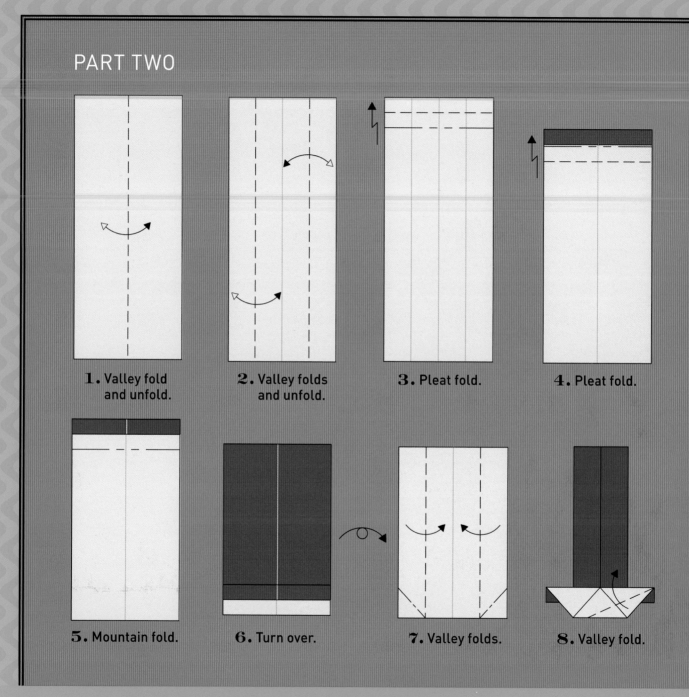

PART TWO

1. Valley fold and unfold.

2. Valley folds and unfold.

3. Pleat fold.

4. Pleat fold.

5. Mountain fold.

6. Turn over.

7. Valley folds.

8. Valley fold.

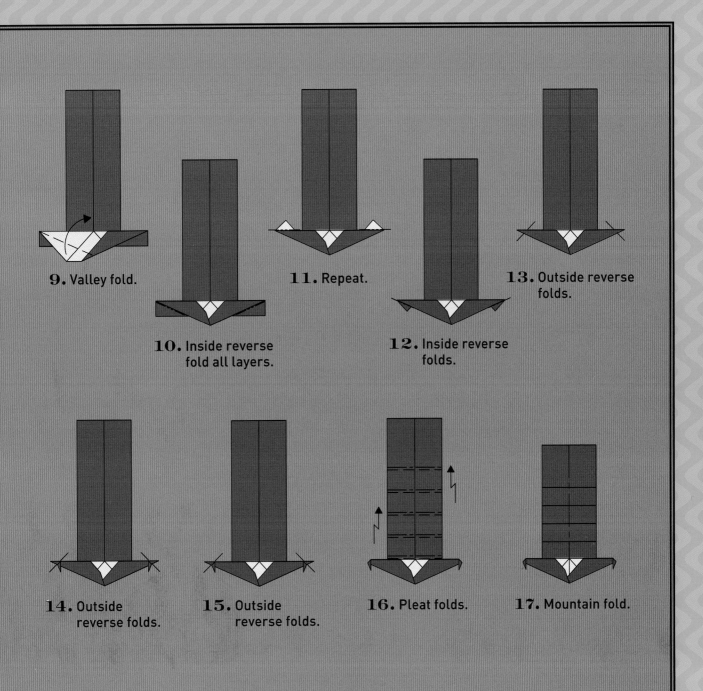

9. Valley fold.

10. Inside reverse fold all layers.

11. Repeat.

12. Inside reverse folds.

13. Outside reverse folds.

14. Outside reverse folds.

15. Outside reverse folds.

16. Pleat folds.

17. Mountain fold.

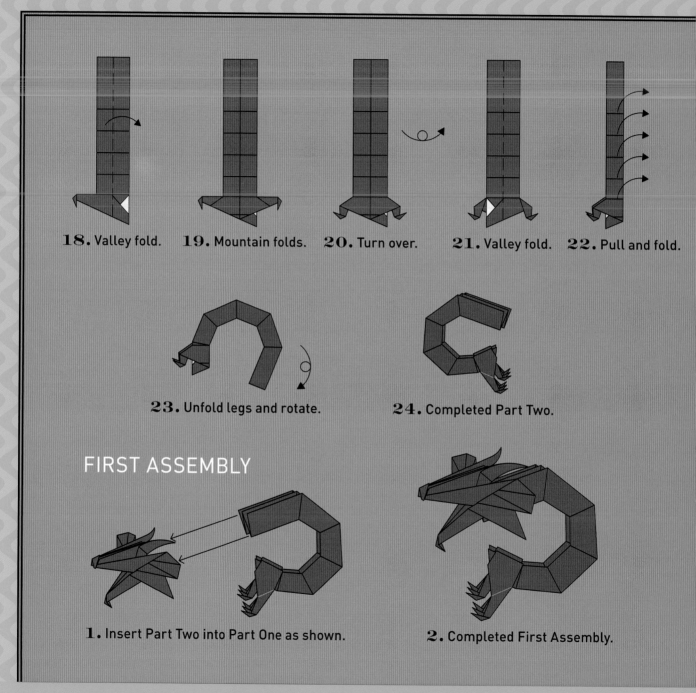

18. Valley fold.　**19.** Mountain folds.　**20.** Turn over.　**21.** Valley fold.　**22.** Pull and fold.

23. Unfold legs and rotate.　　**24.** Completed Part Two.

FIRST ASSEMBLY

1. Insert Part Two into Part One as shown.　　**2.** Completed First Assembly.

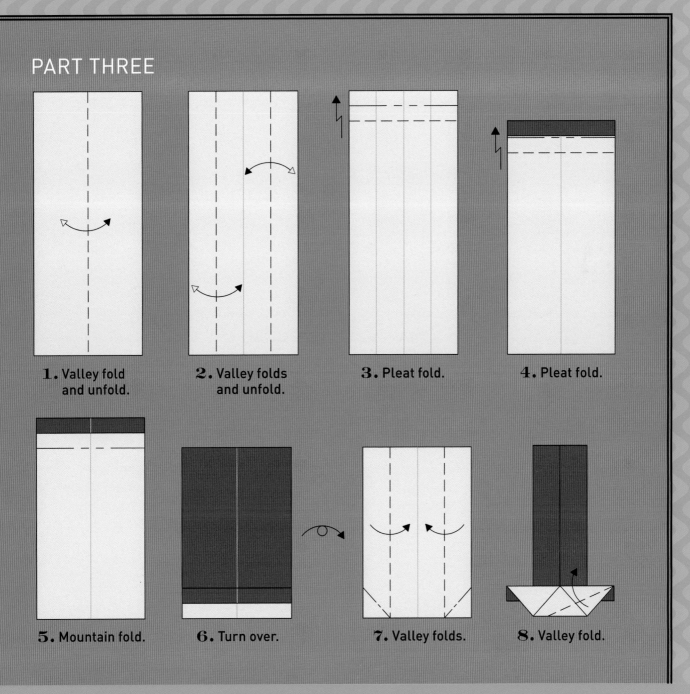

PART THREE

1. Valley fold and unfold.

2. Valley folds and unfold.

3. Pleat fold.

4. Pleat fold.

5. Mountain fold.

6. Turn over.

7. Valley folds.

8. Valley fold.

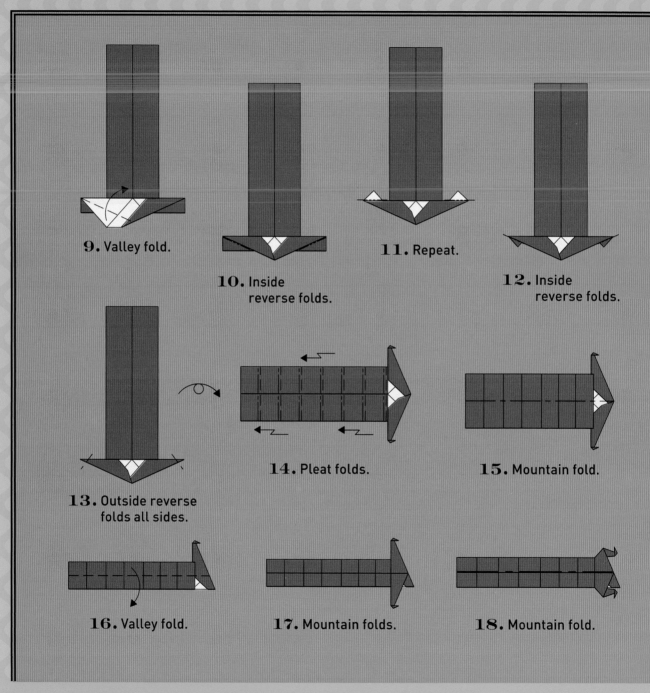

9. Valley fold.

10. Inside reverse folds.

11. Repeat.

12. Inside reverse folds.

13. Outside reverse folds all sides.

14. Pleat folds.

15. Mountain fold.

16. Valley fold.

17. Mountain folds.

18. Mountain fold.

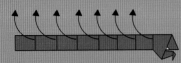

19. Pull and fold.

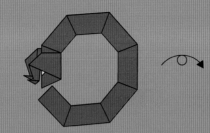

20. Unfold legs and rotate.

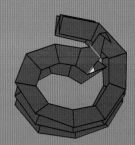

21. Completed Part Three.

SECOND ASSEMBLY

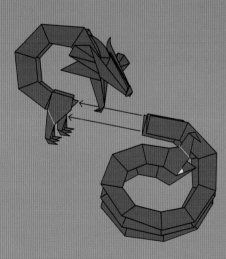

1. Attach First Assembly and Part Three.

PART FOUR

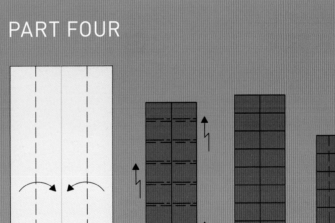

1. Valley folds.

2. Pleat folds.

3. Valley folds.

4. Valley folds.

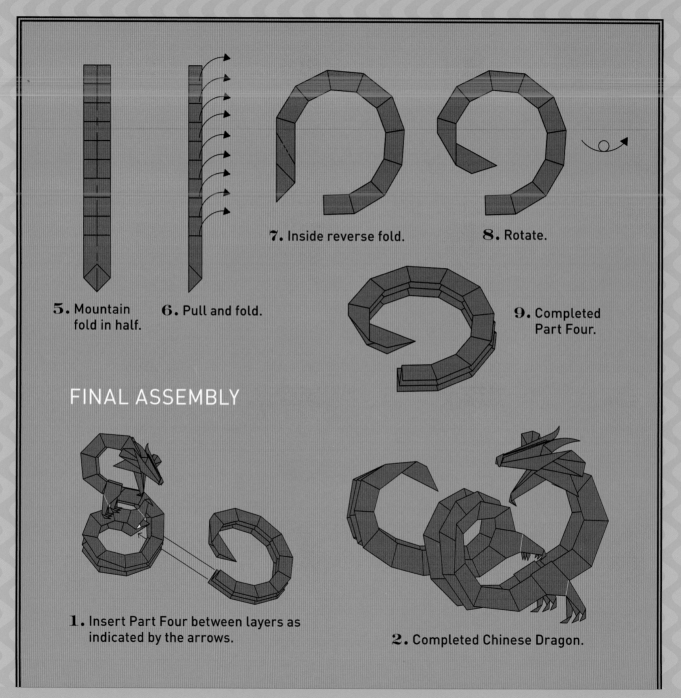

5. Mountain fold in half.

6. Pull and fold.

7. Inside reverse fold.

8. Rotate.

9. Completed Part Four.

FINAL ASSEMBLY

1. Insert Part Four between layers as indicated by the arrows.

2. Completed Chinese Dragon.